Tracing

	A	B	C	D	E	F
1						
2						
3						
4						
5						
6						
7						

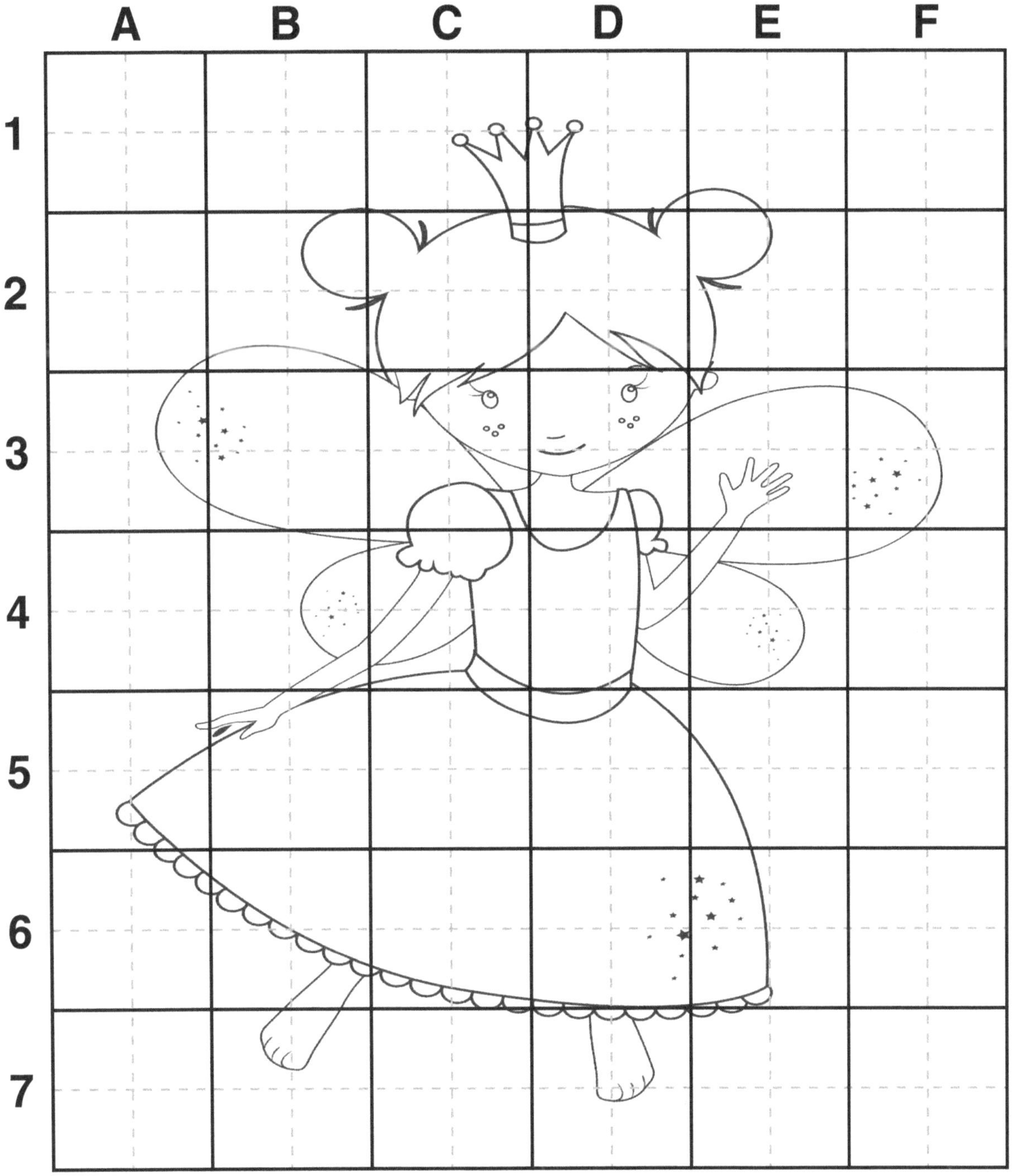

Your tract!

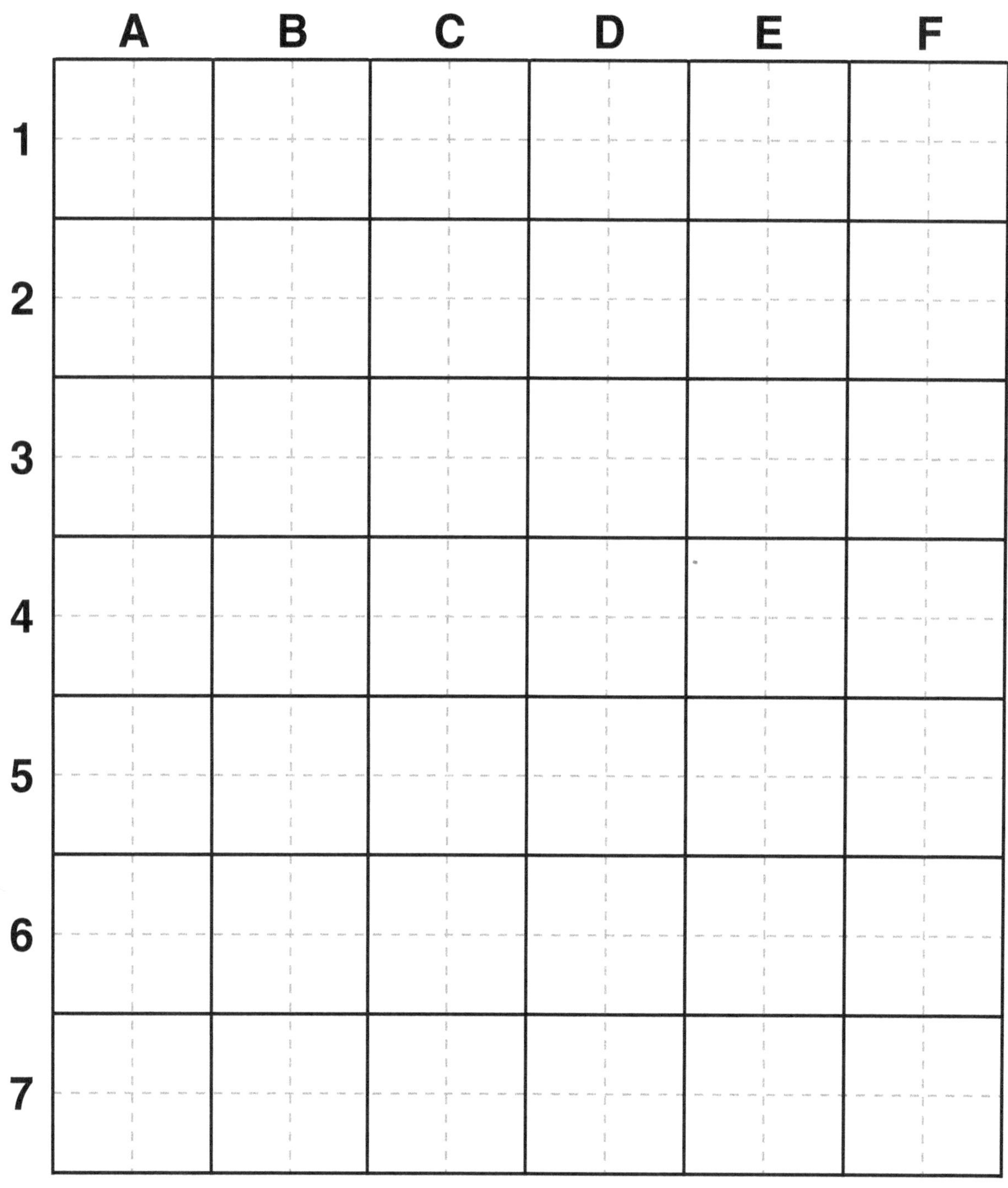

Coloring

Practice!

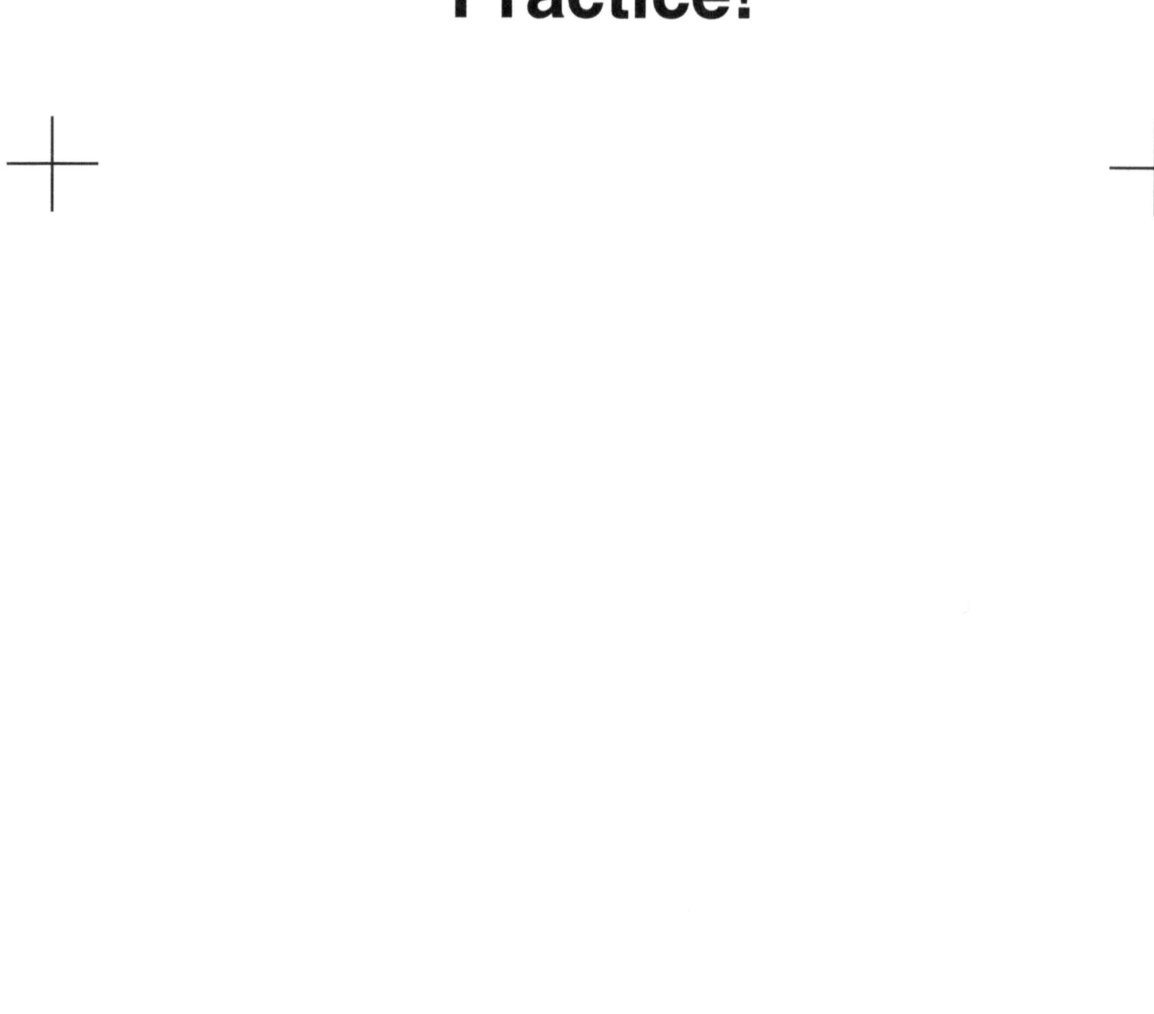

Make perfect!

Tracing

Your tract!

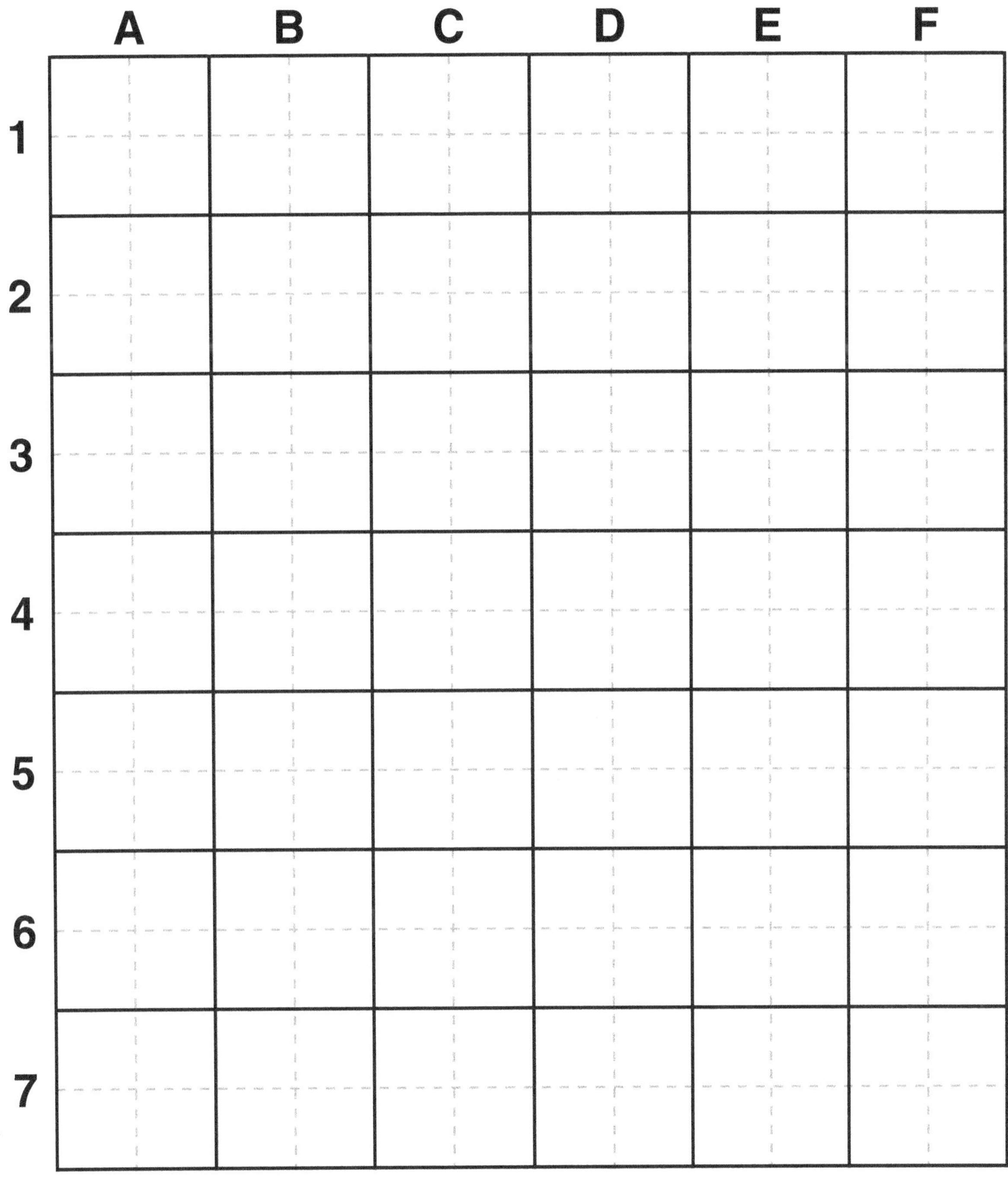

Coloring

Practice!

Make perfect!

Tracing

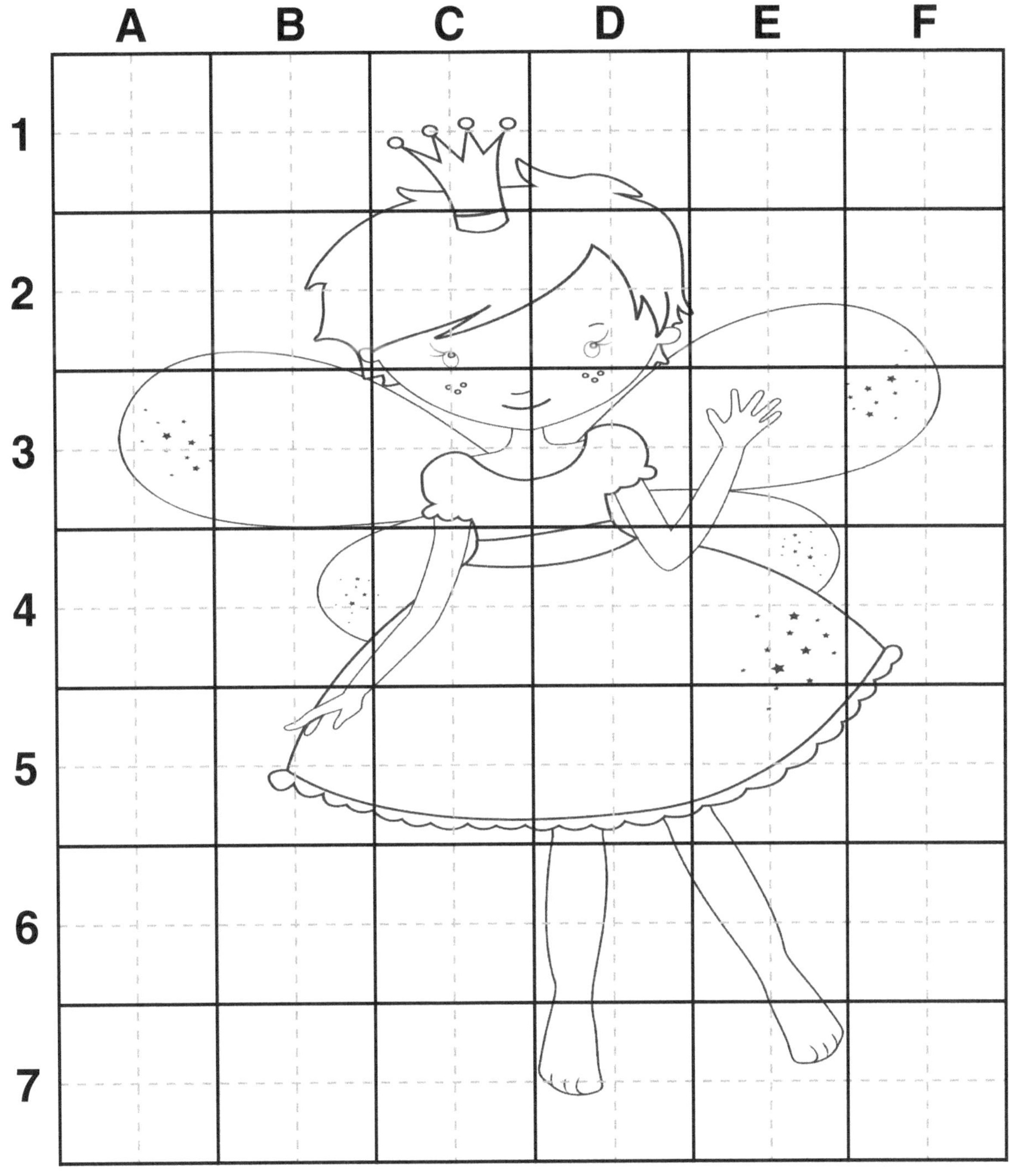

Your tract!

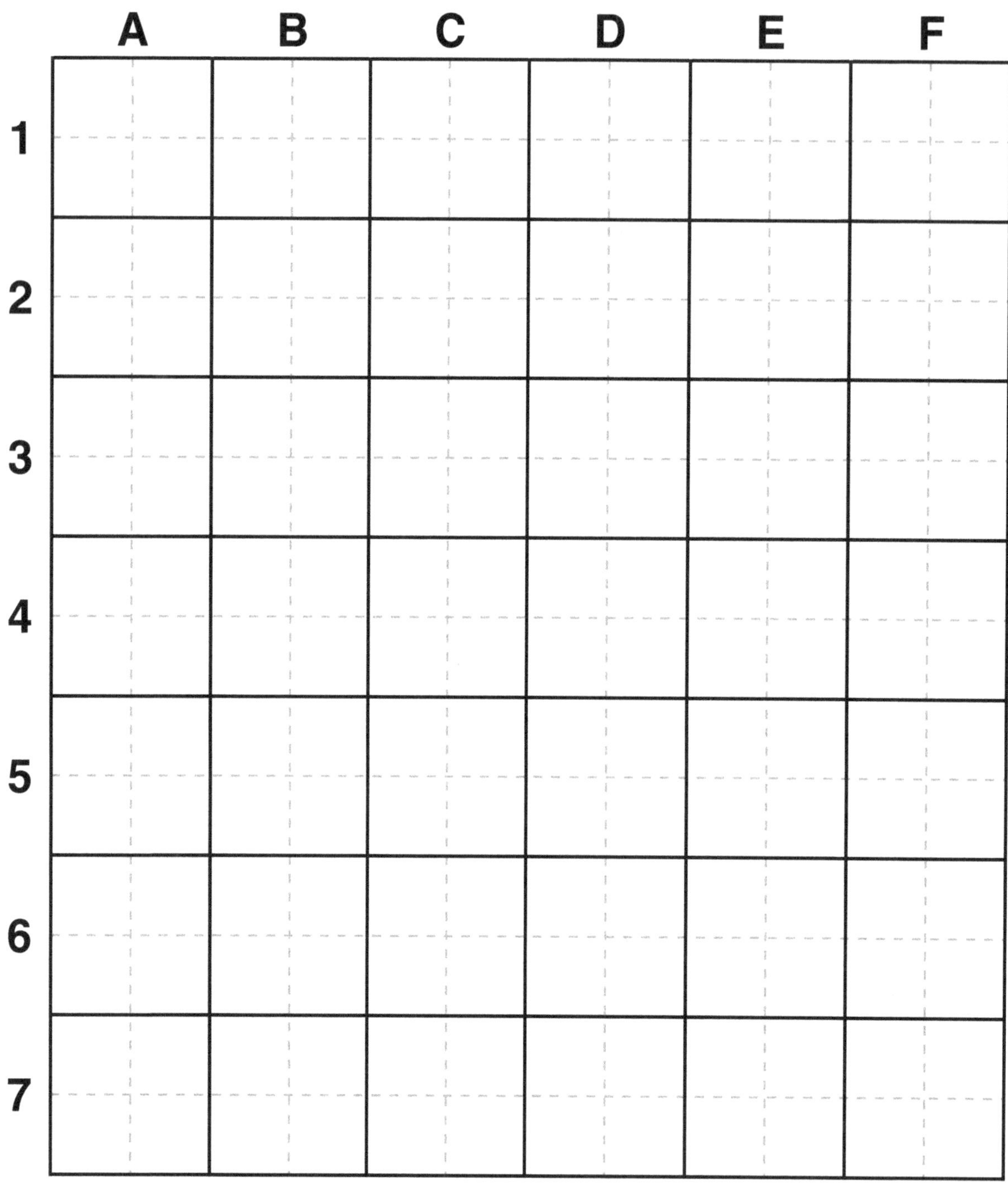

Coloring

Practice!

Make perfect!

Tracing

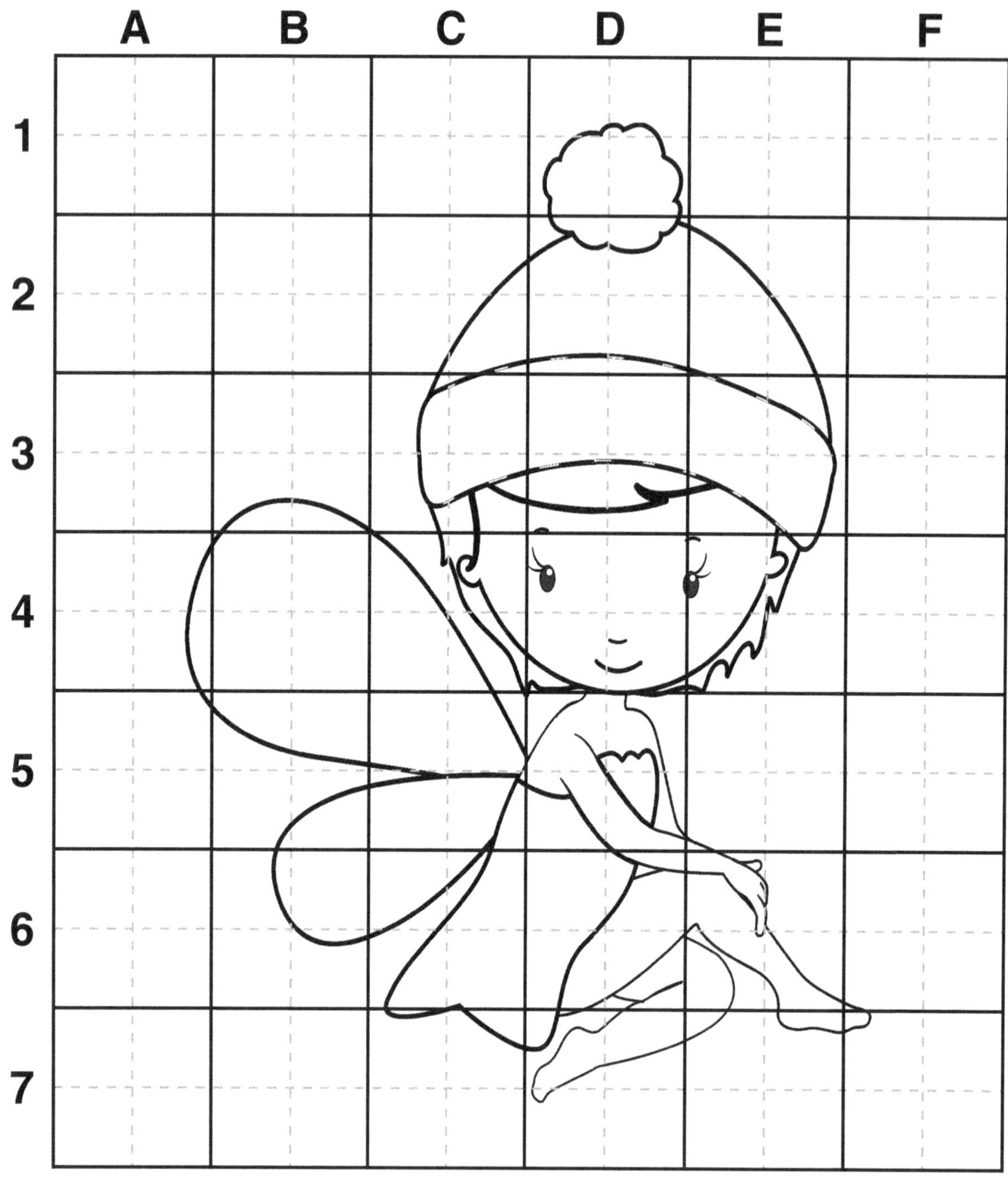

Your tract!

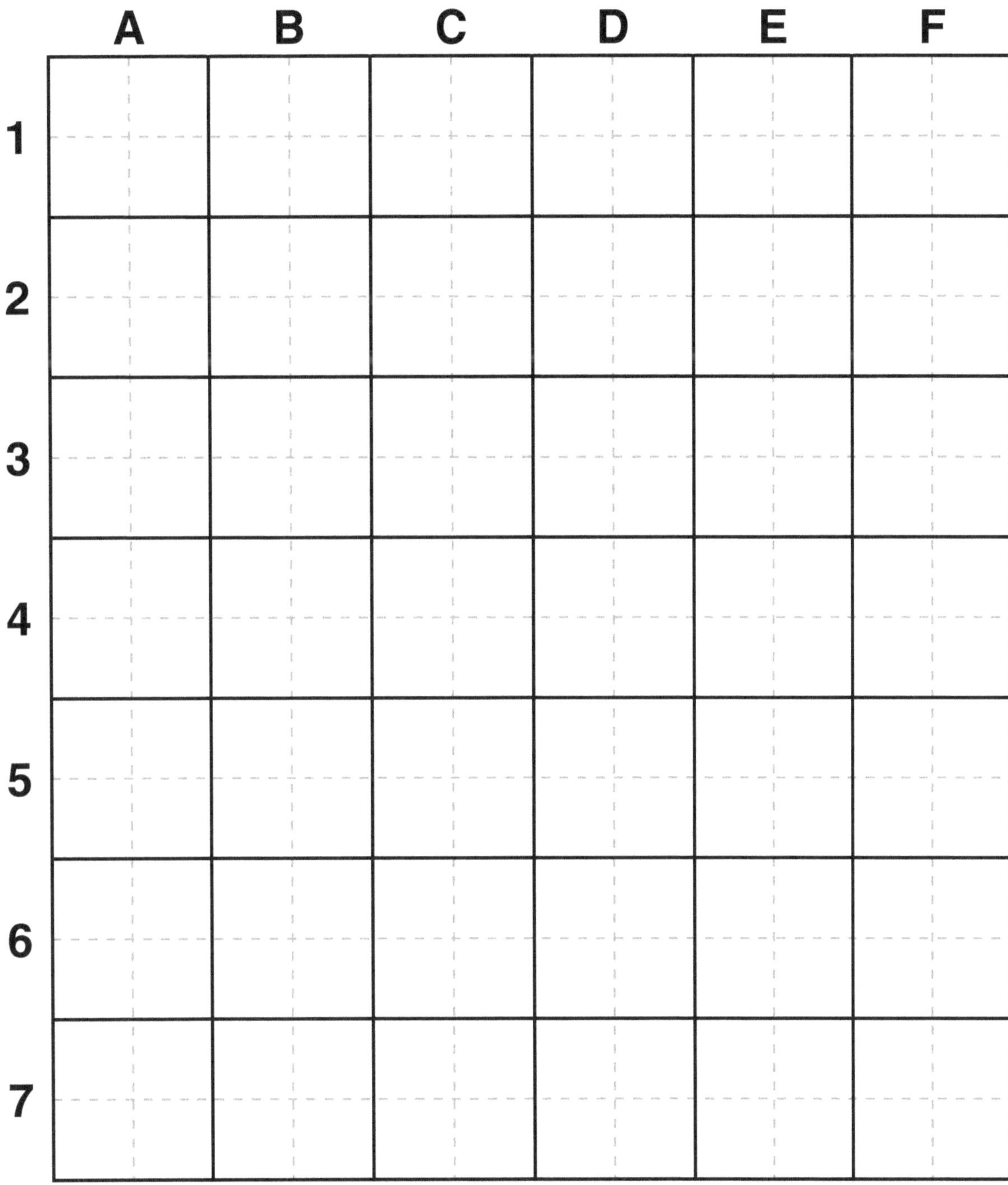

Coloring

Practice!

Make perfect!

Tracing

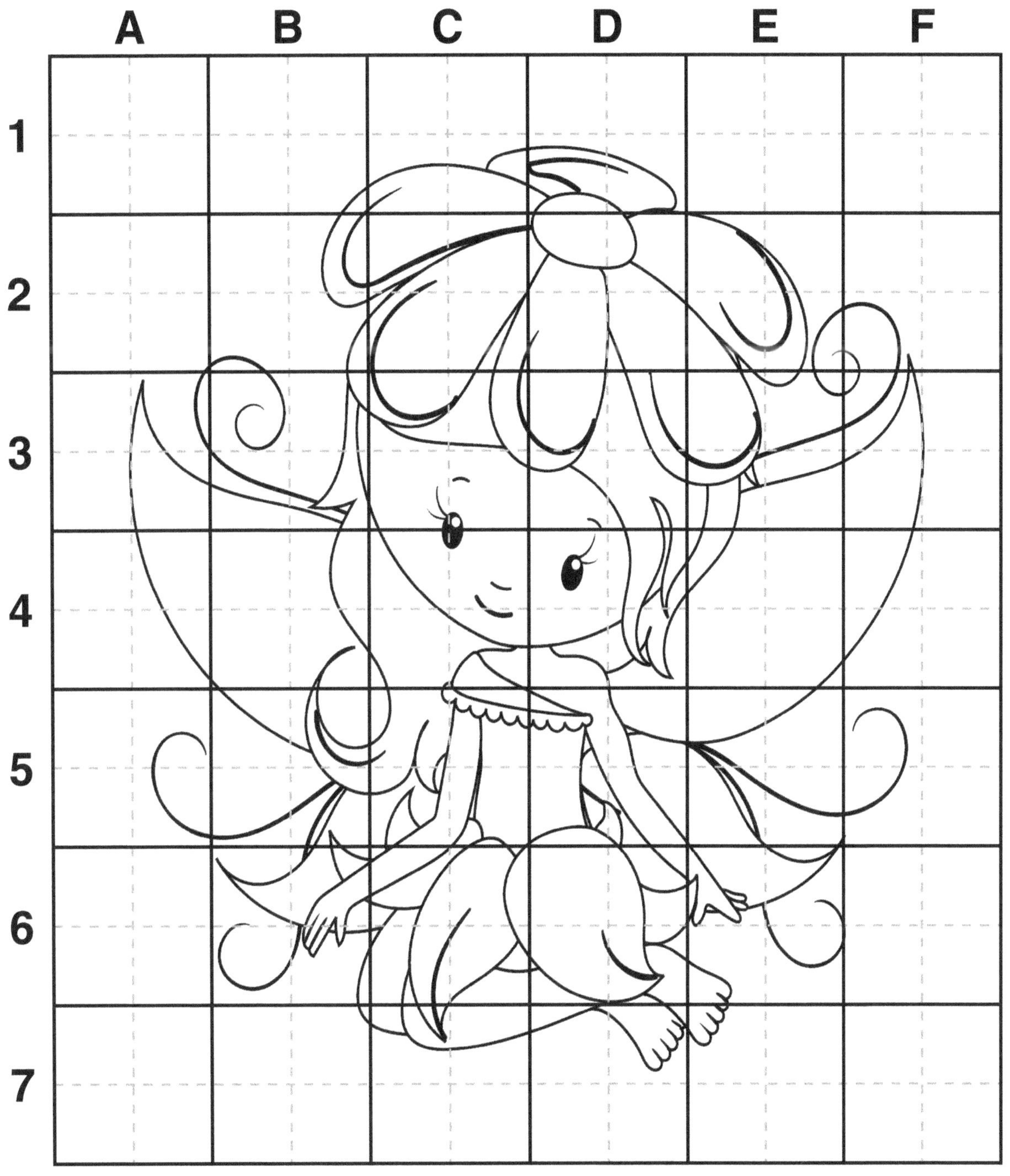

Your tract!

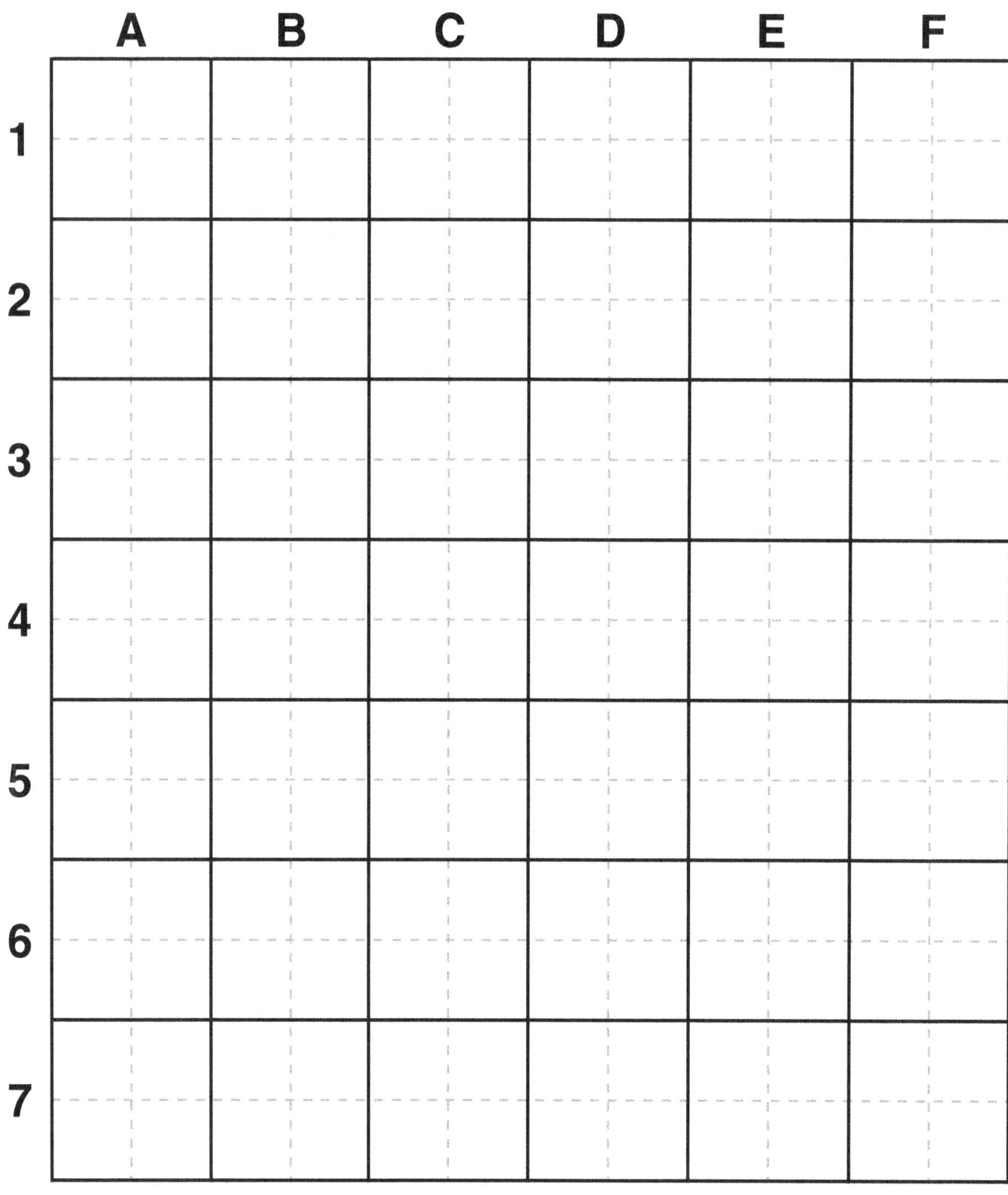

Coloring

Practice!

Make perfect!

Tracing

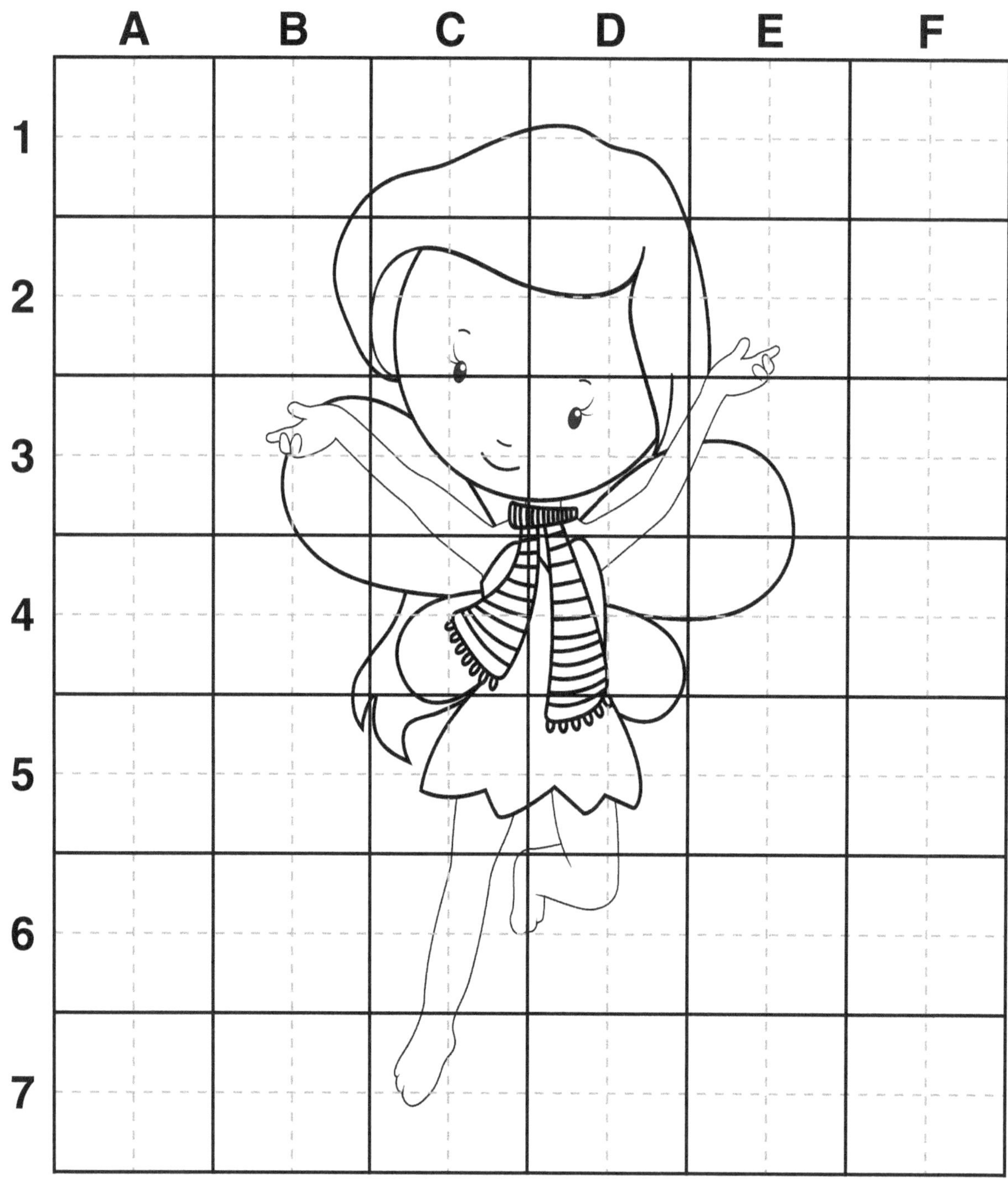

Your tract!

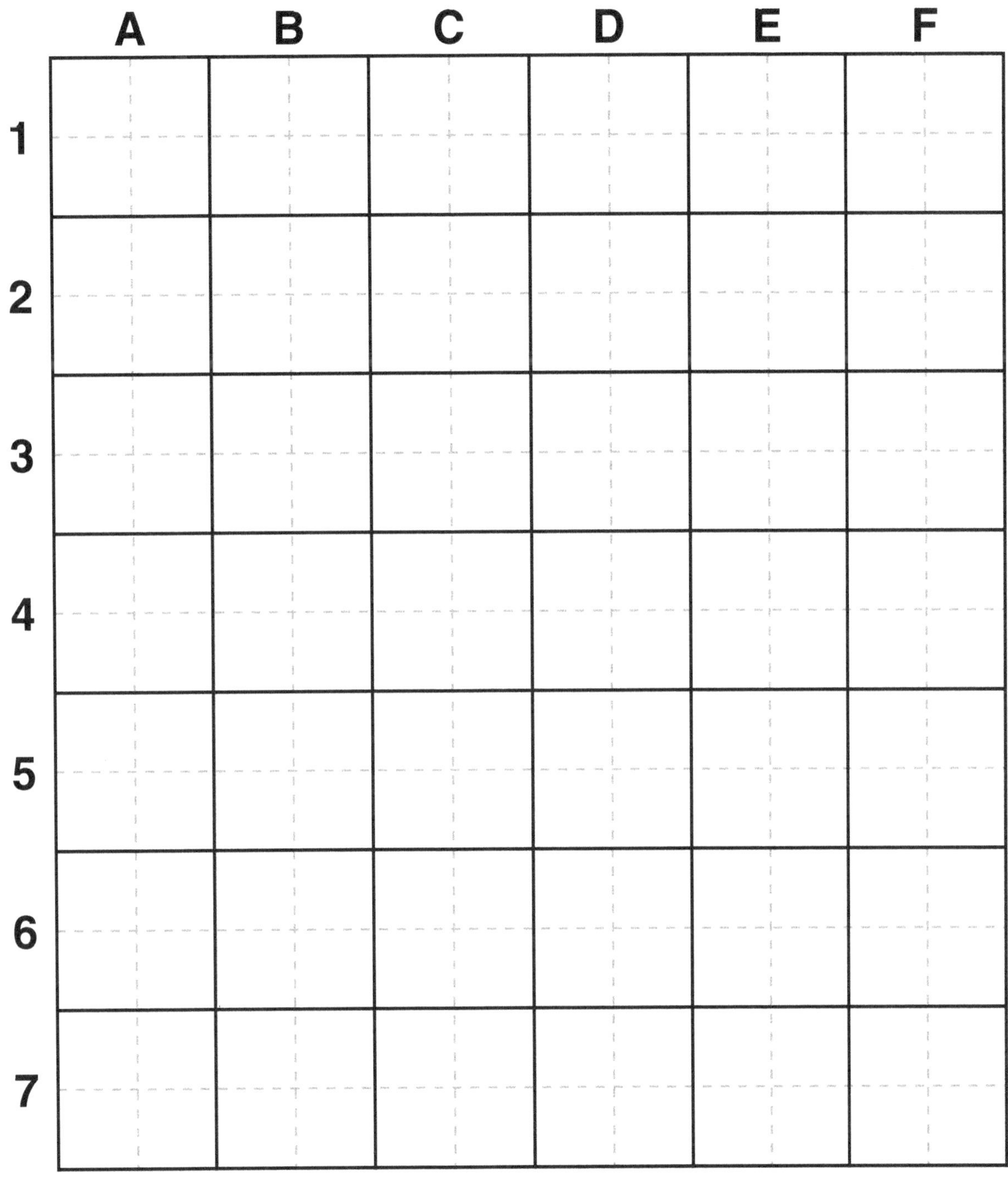

Coloring

Practice!

Make perfect!

Tracing

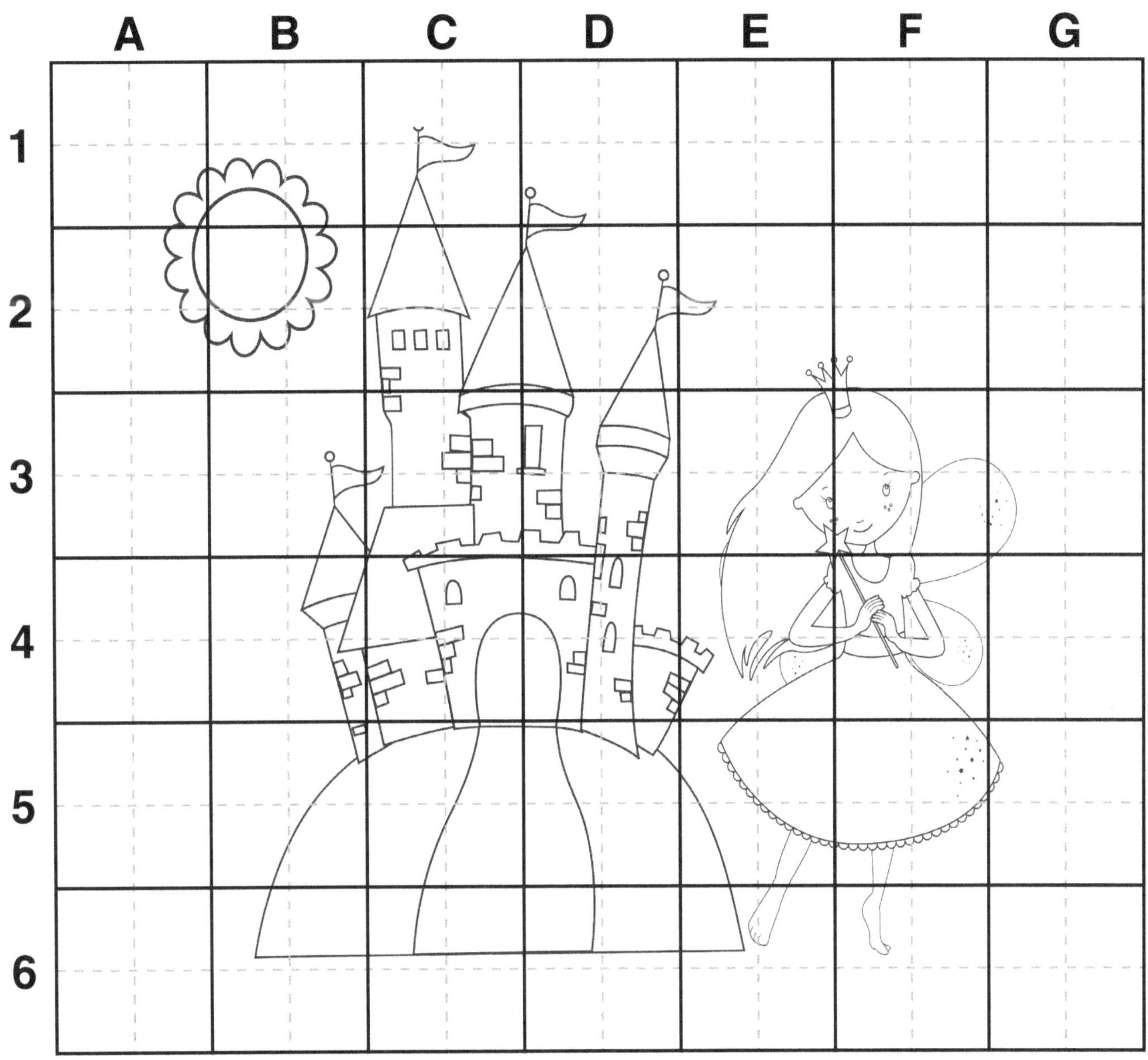

Your tract!

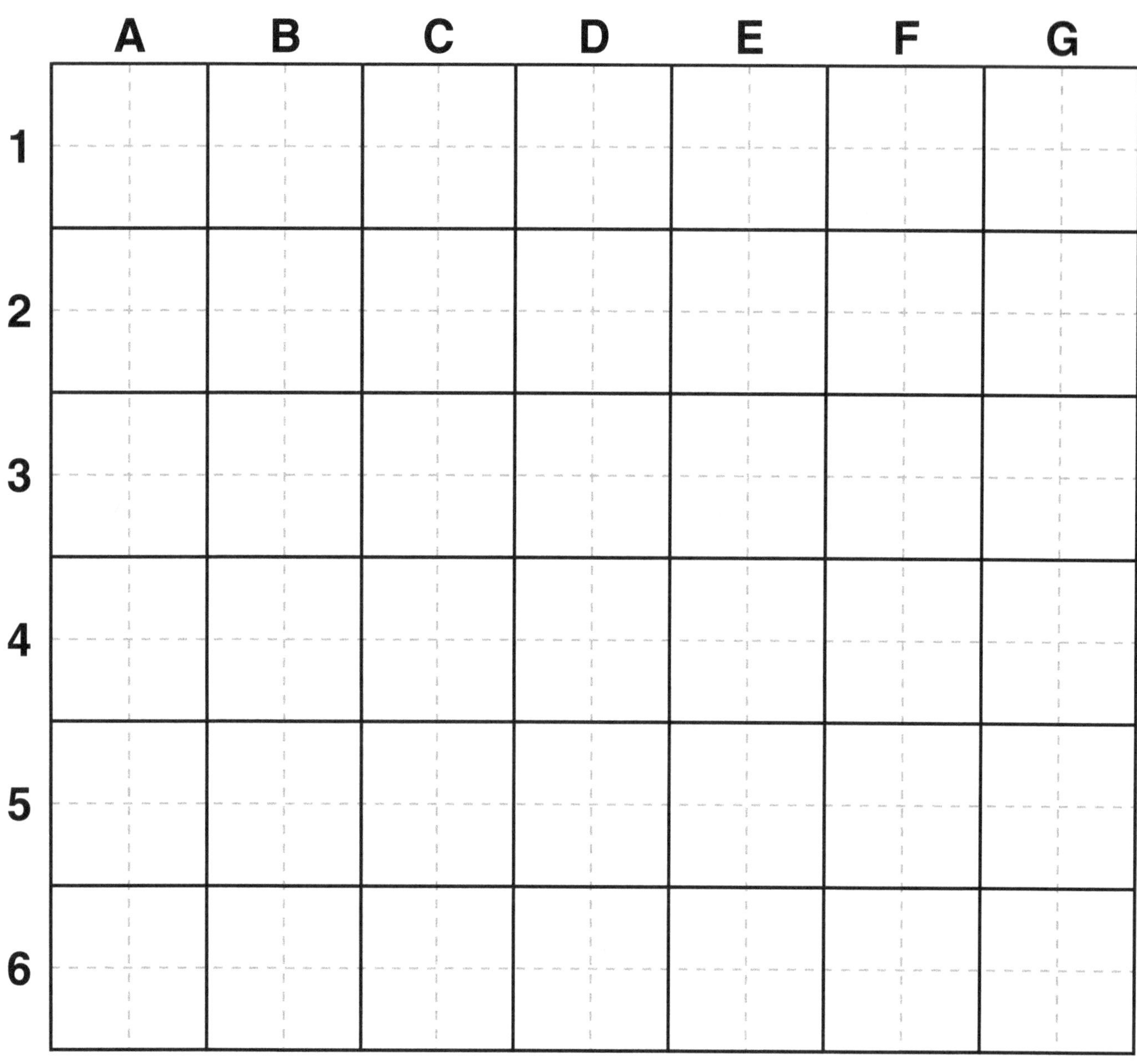

Coloring

Practice!

Make perfect!

Tracing

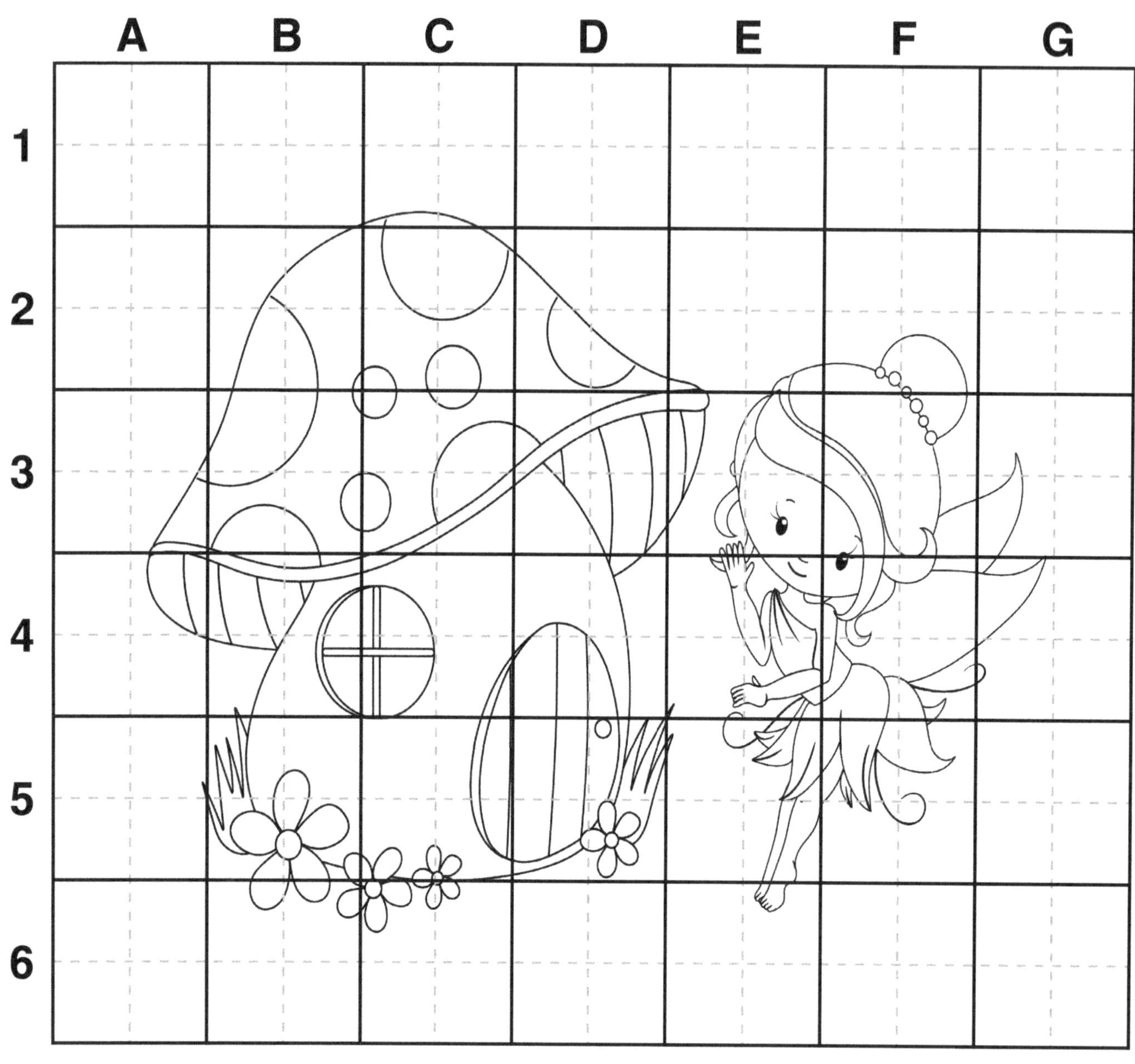

Your tract!

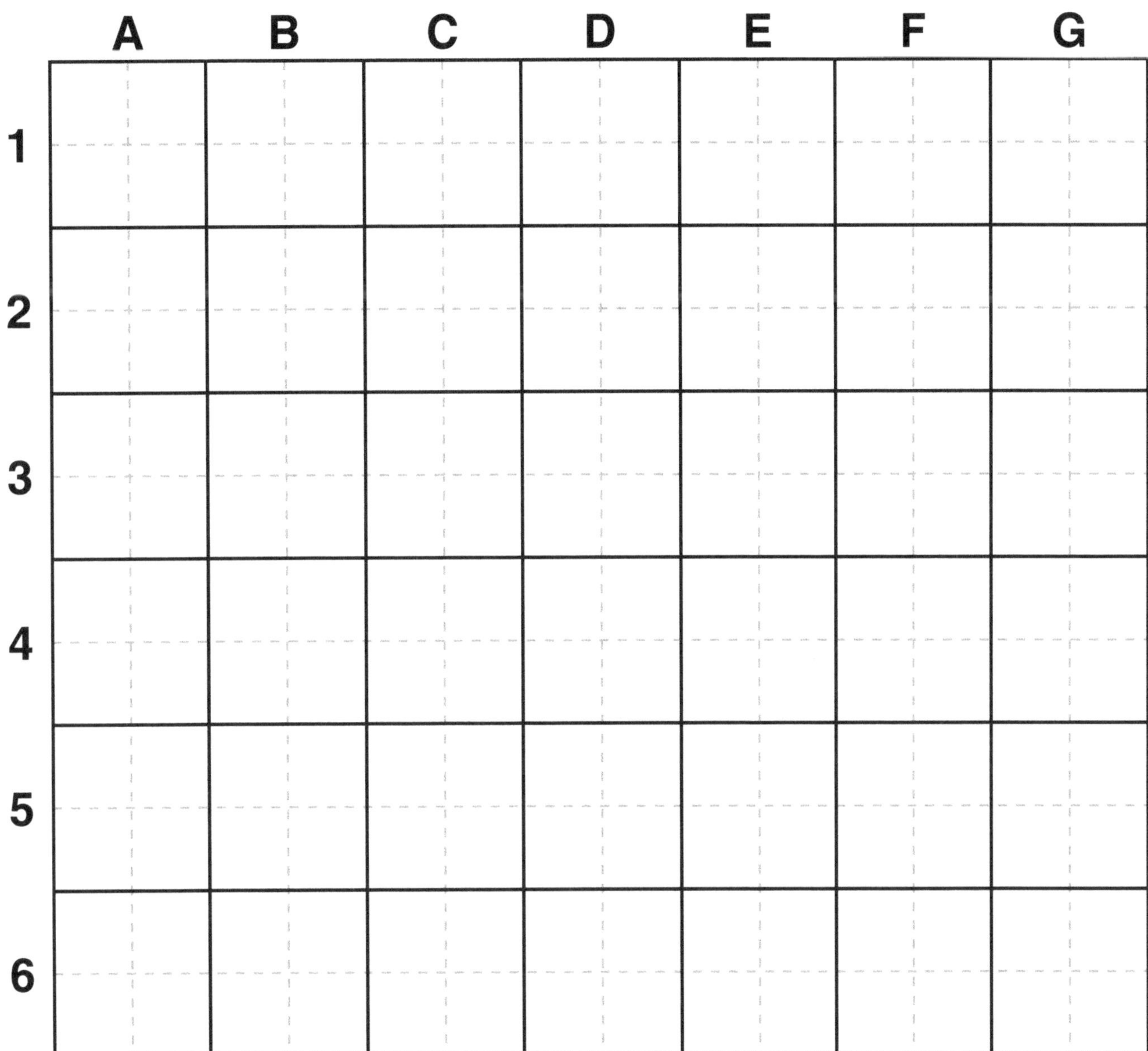

Coloring

Practice!

Make perfect!

Tracing

Your tract!

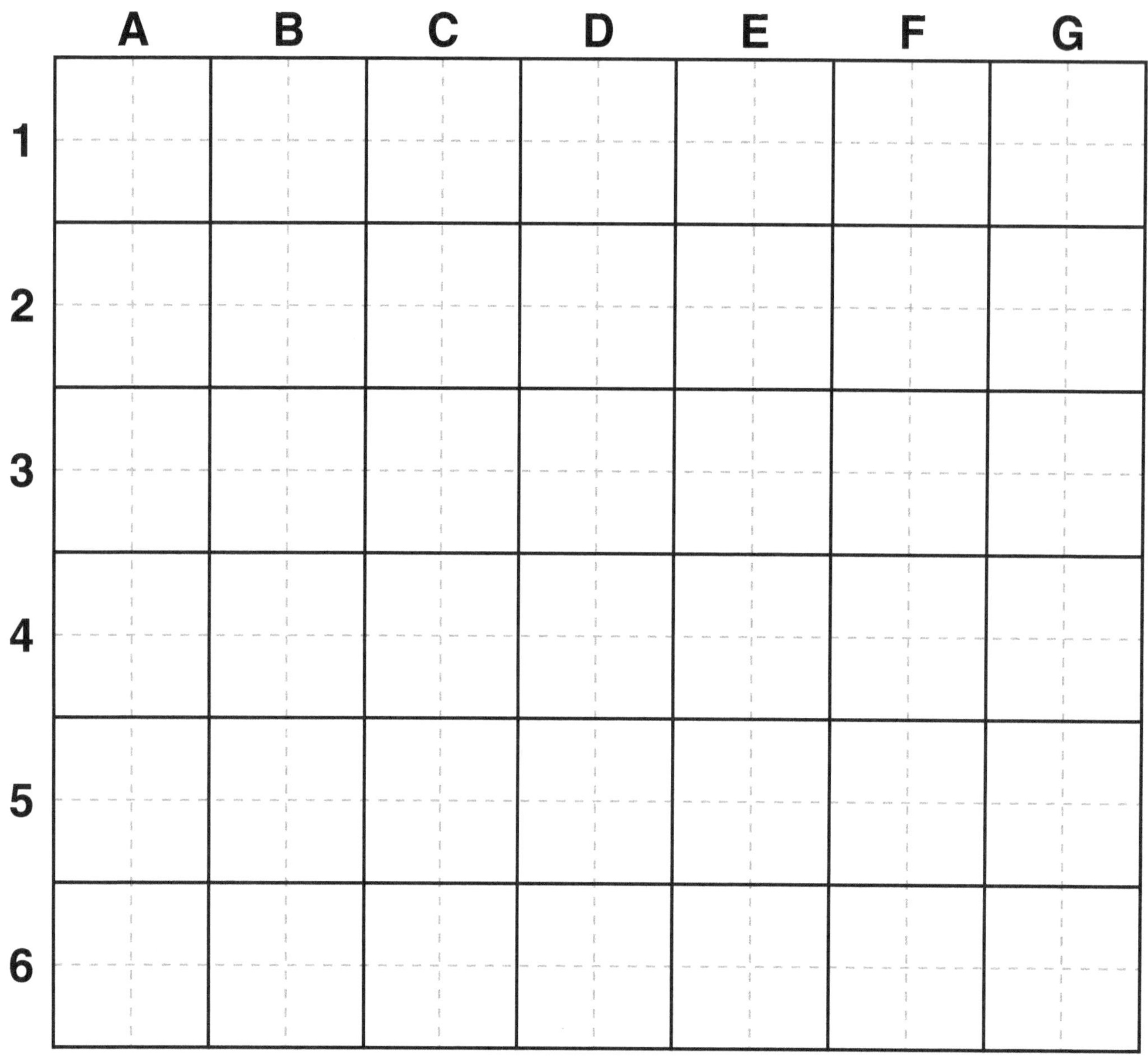

Coloring

Practice!

Make perfect!

Tracing

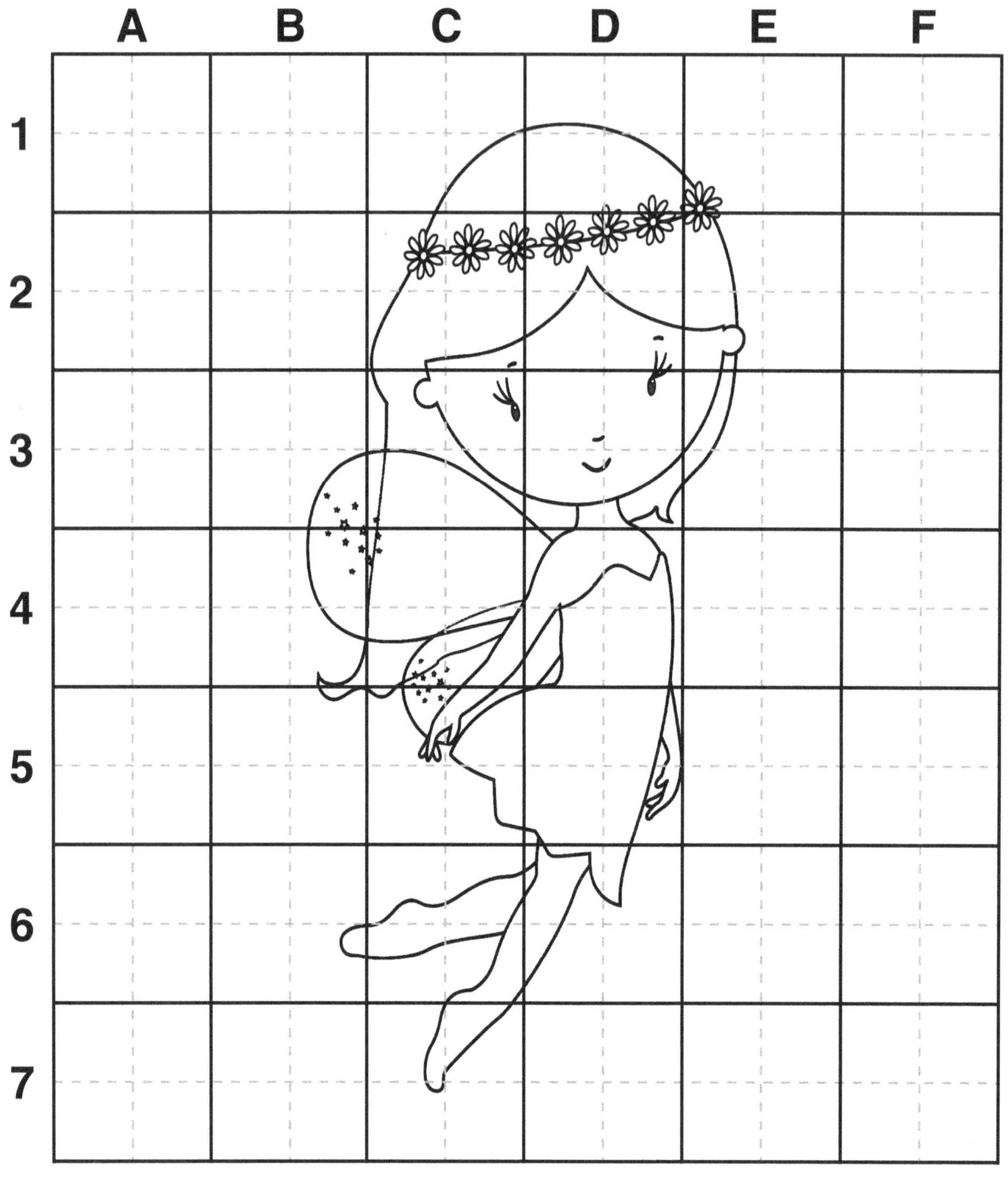

Your tract!

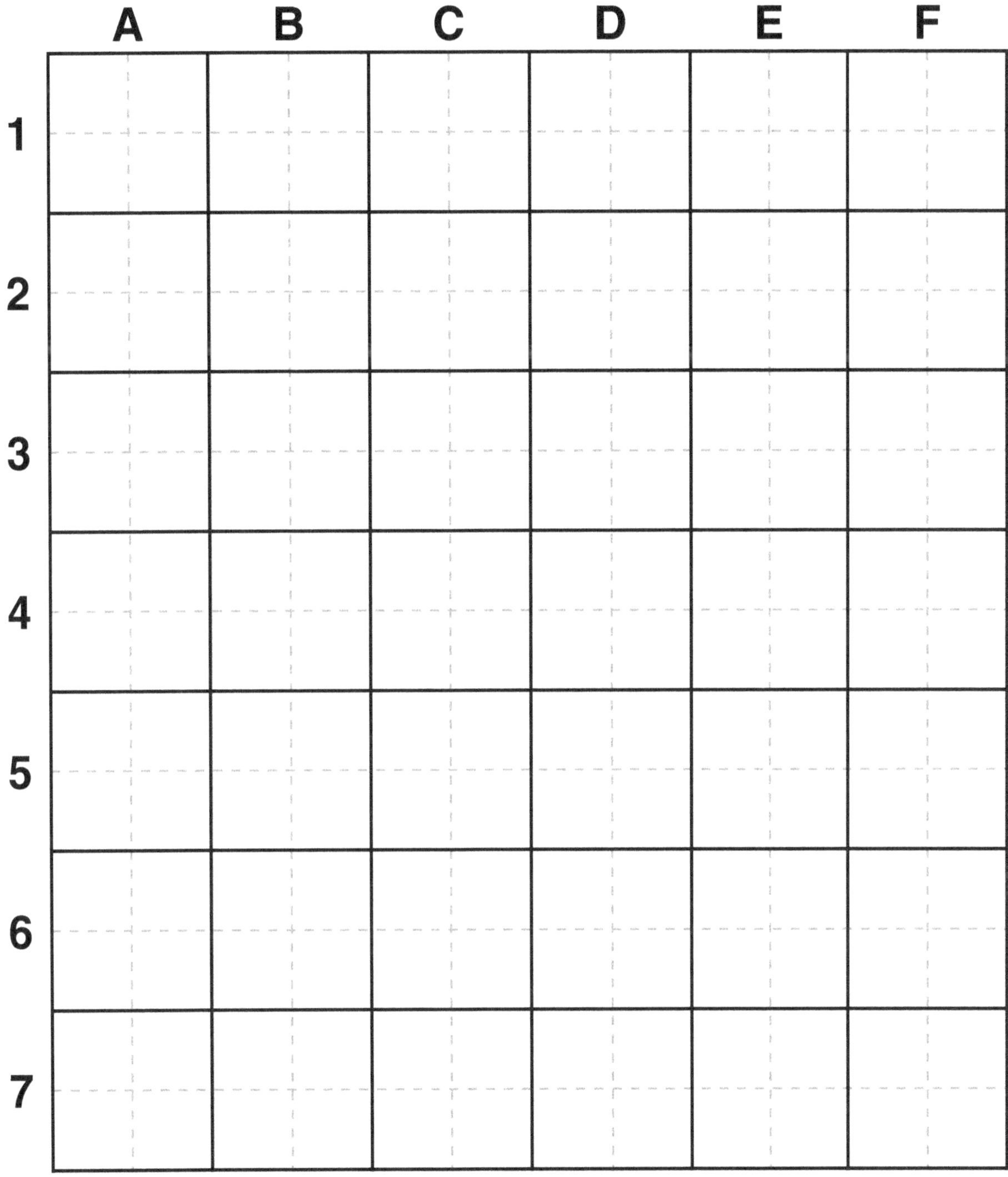

Coloring

Practice!

Make perfect!

Tracing

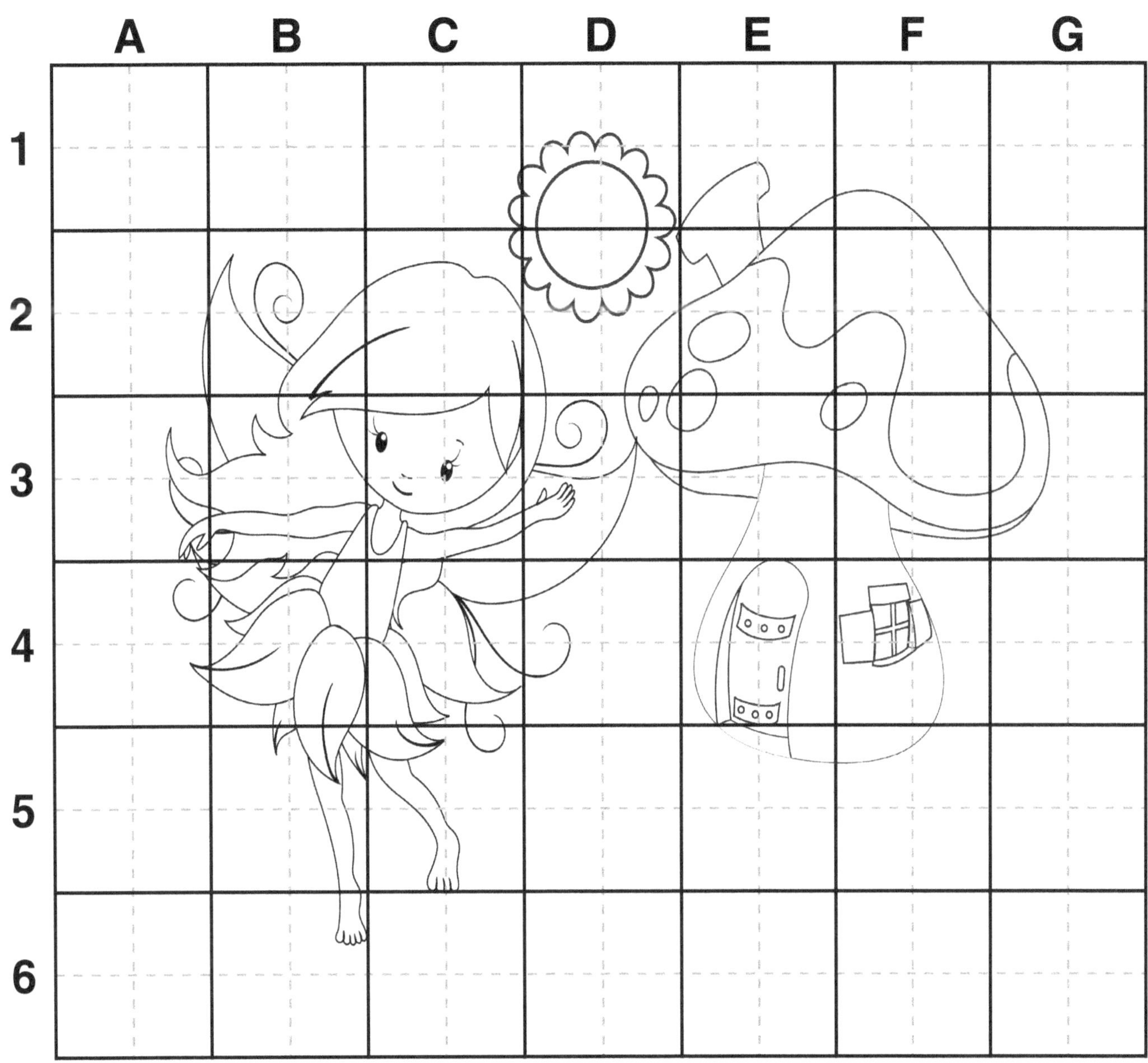

Your tract!

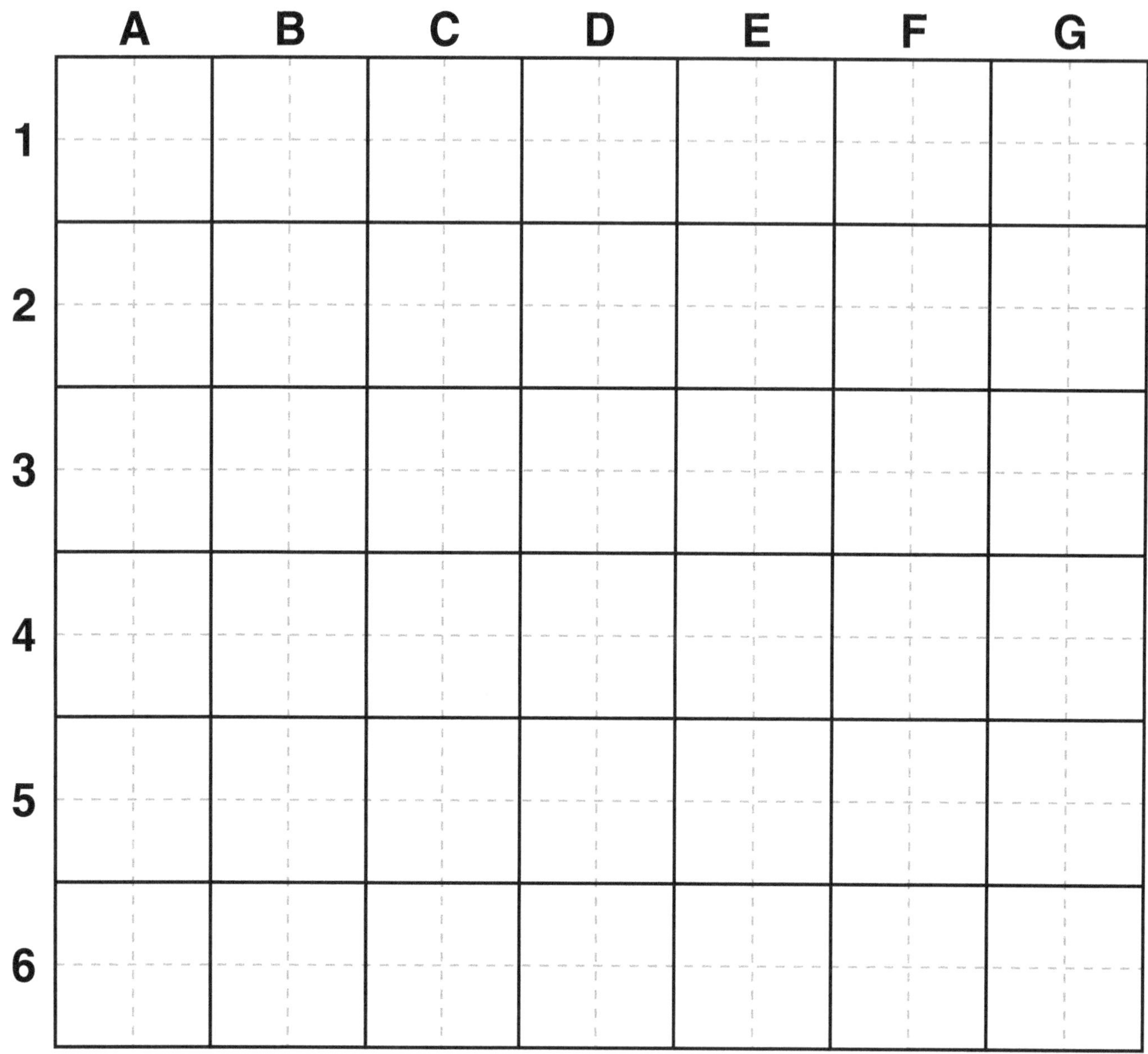

Coloring

Practice!

Make perfect!

Tracing

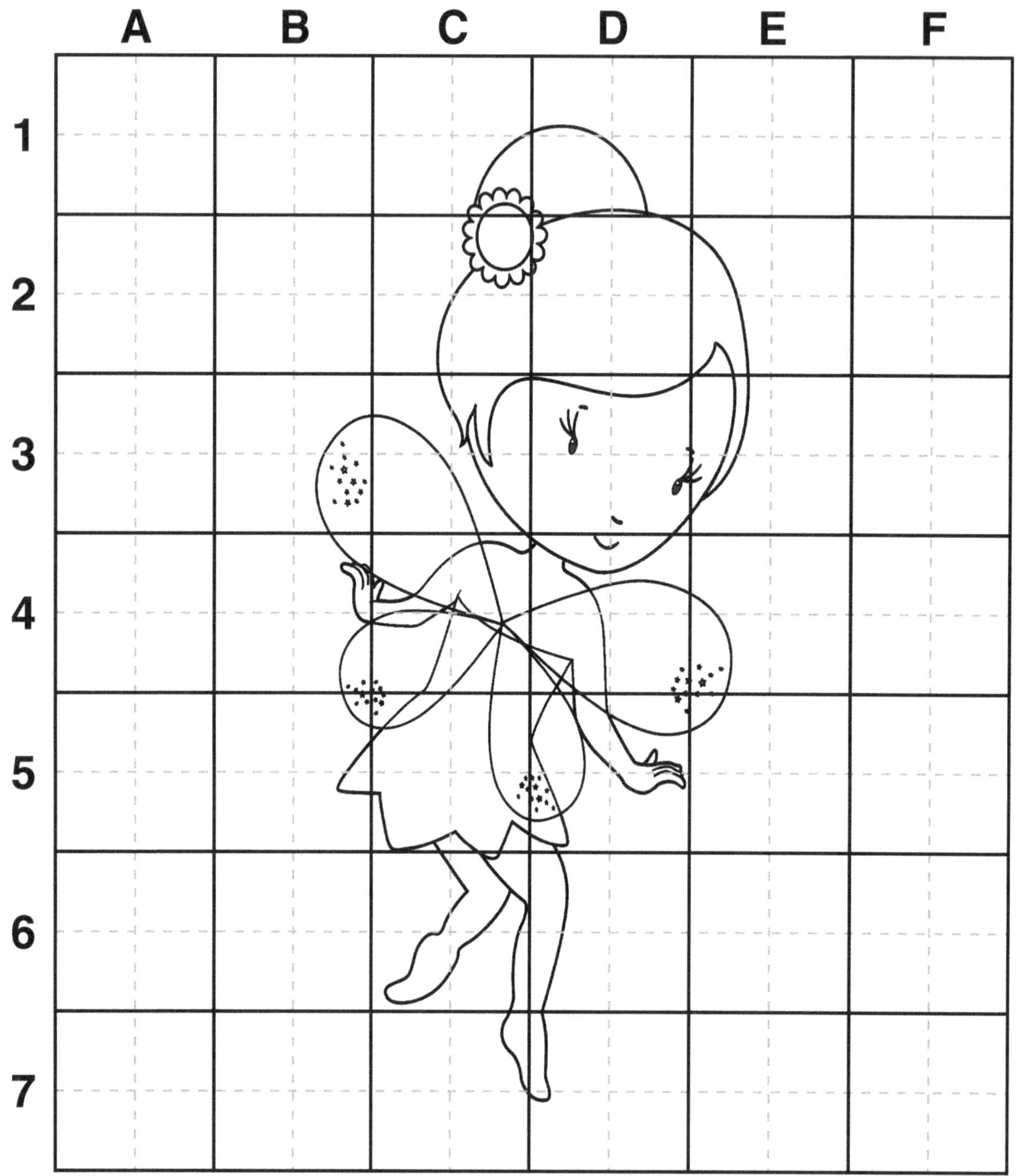

Your tract!

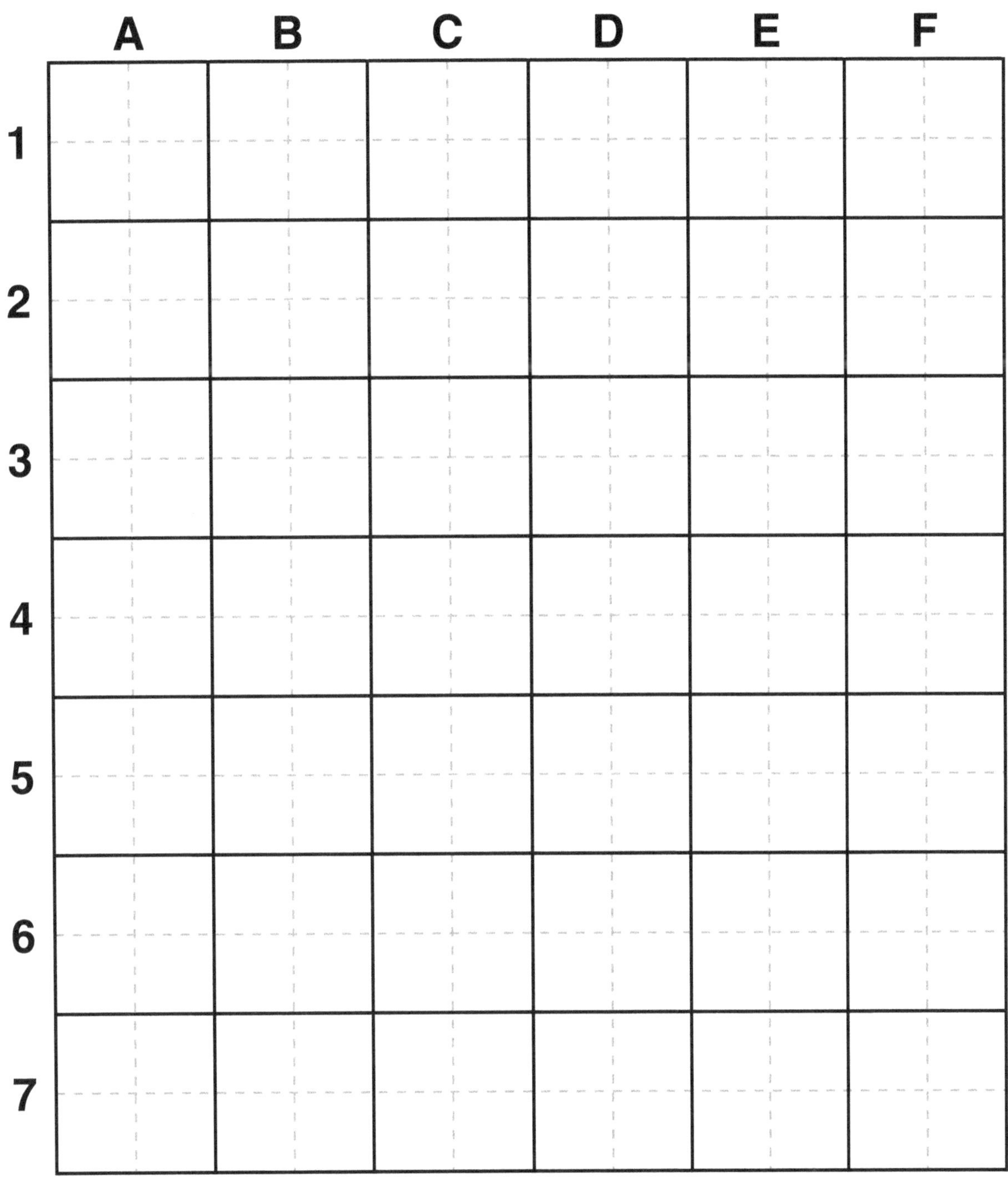

Coloring

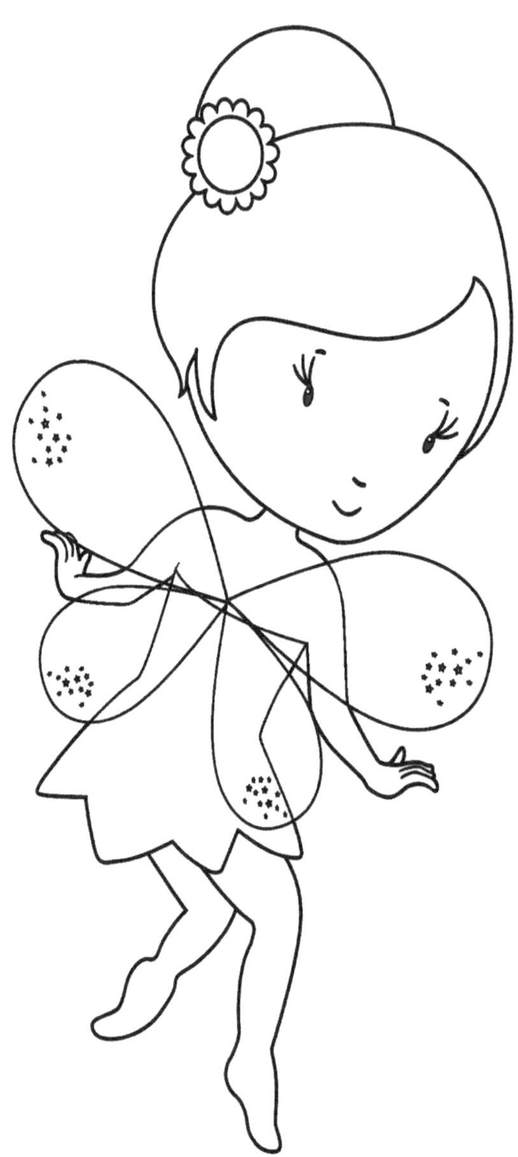

Practice!

Make perfect!

Tracing

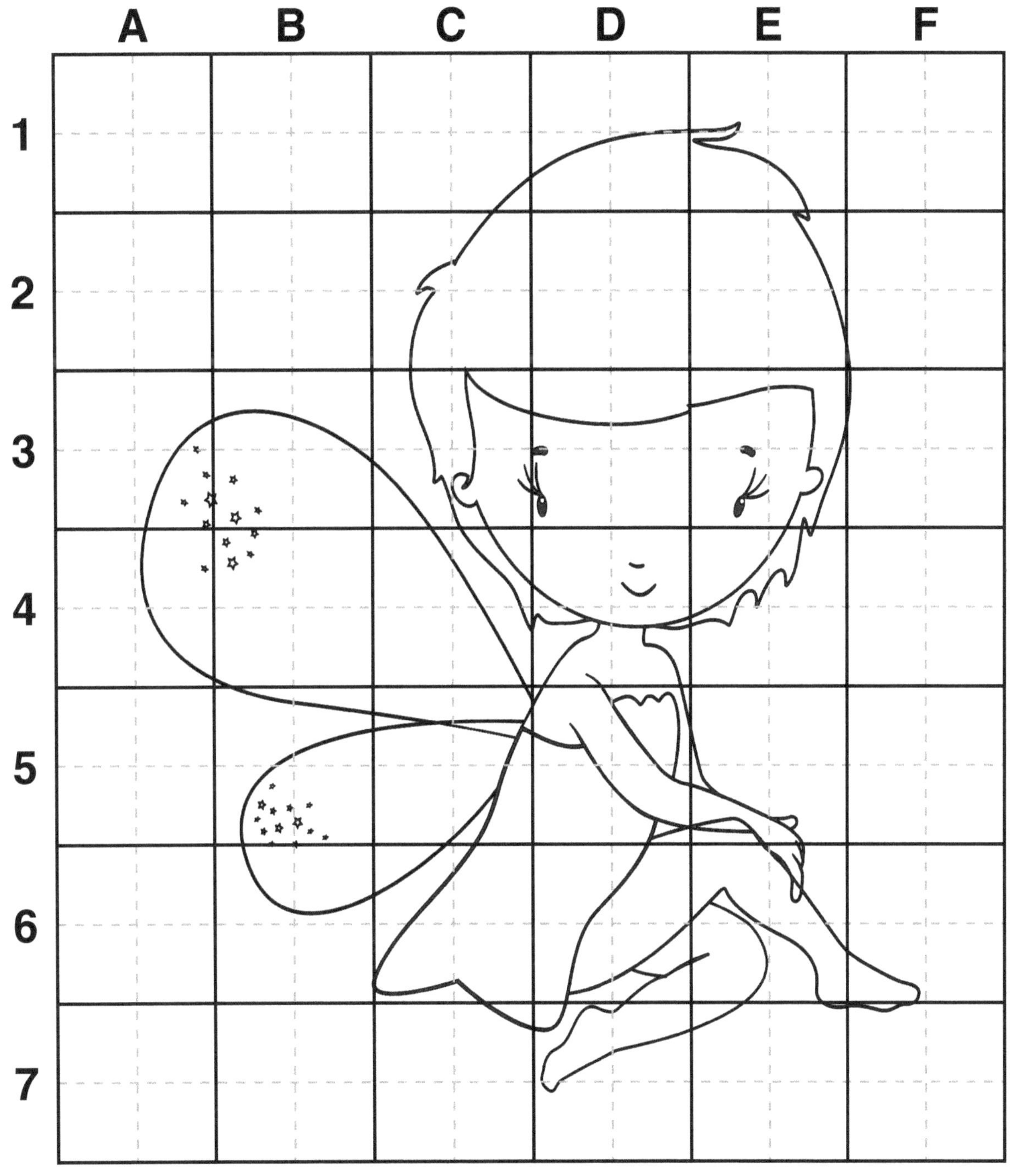

Your tract!

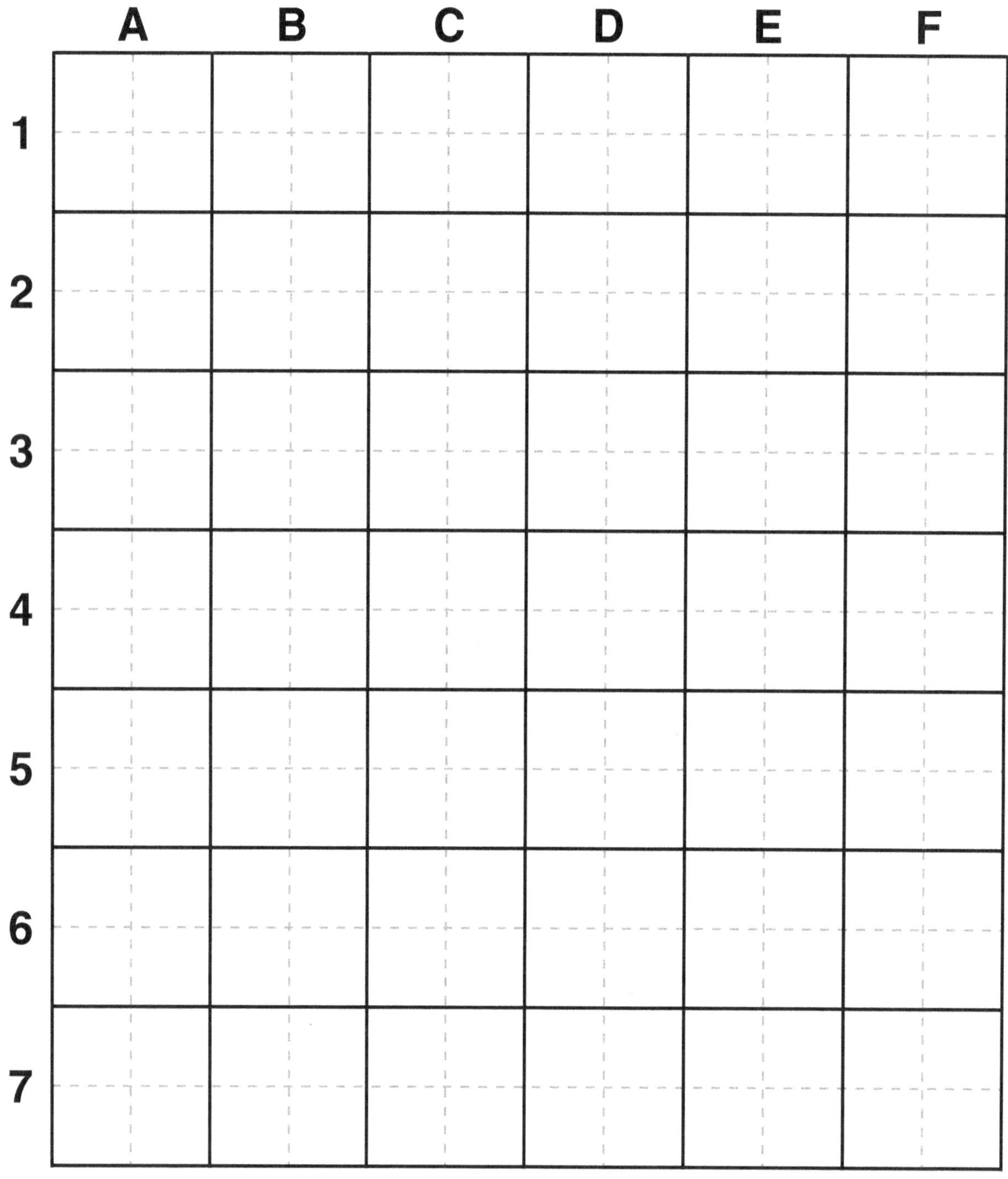

Coloring

Practice!

Make perfect!

Tracing

Your tract!

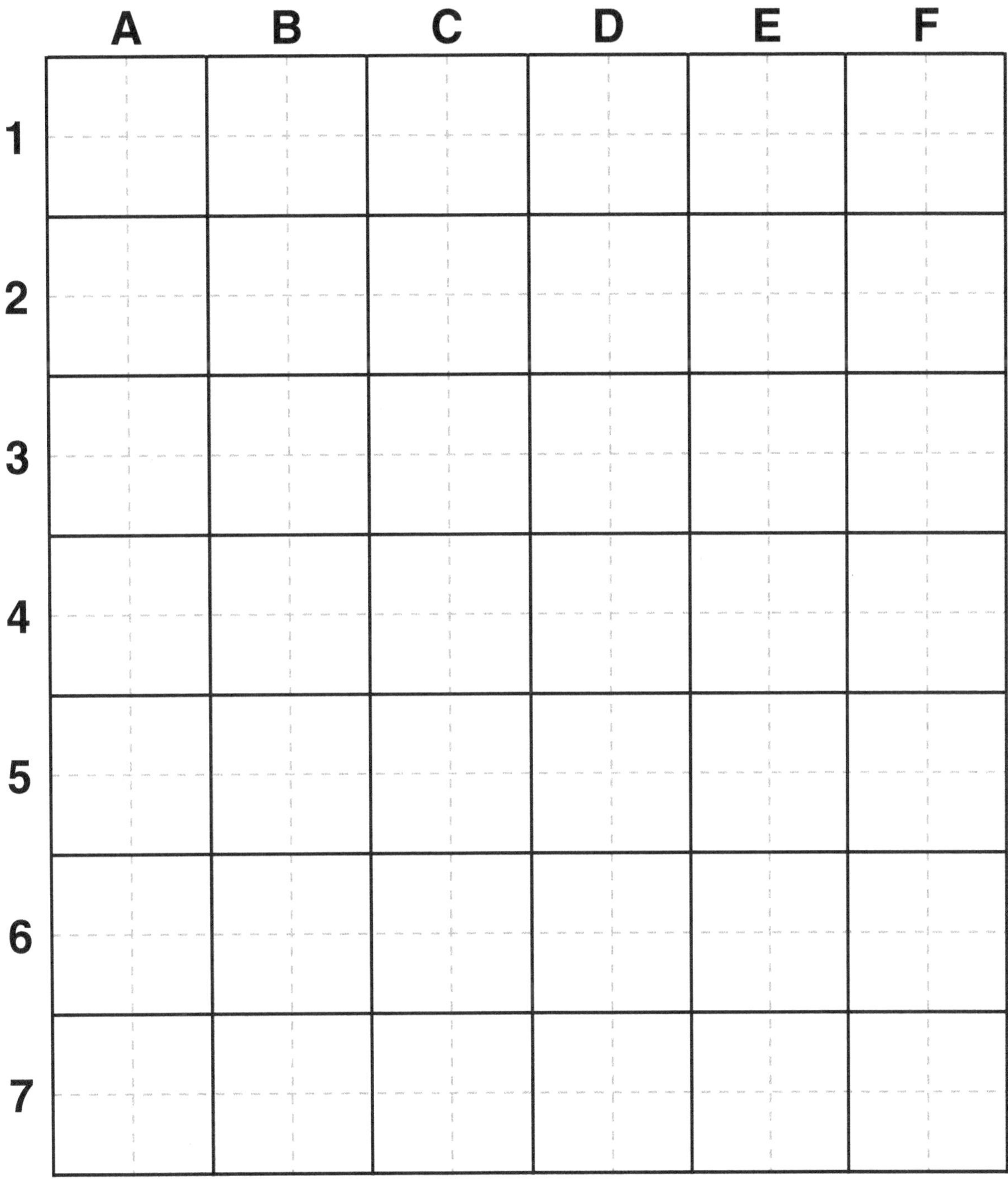

Coloring

Practice!

Make perfect!

Tracing

Your tract!

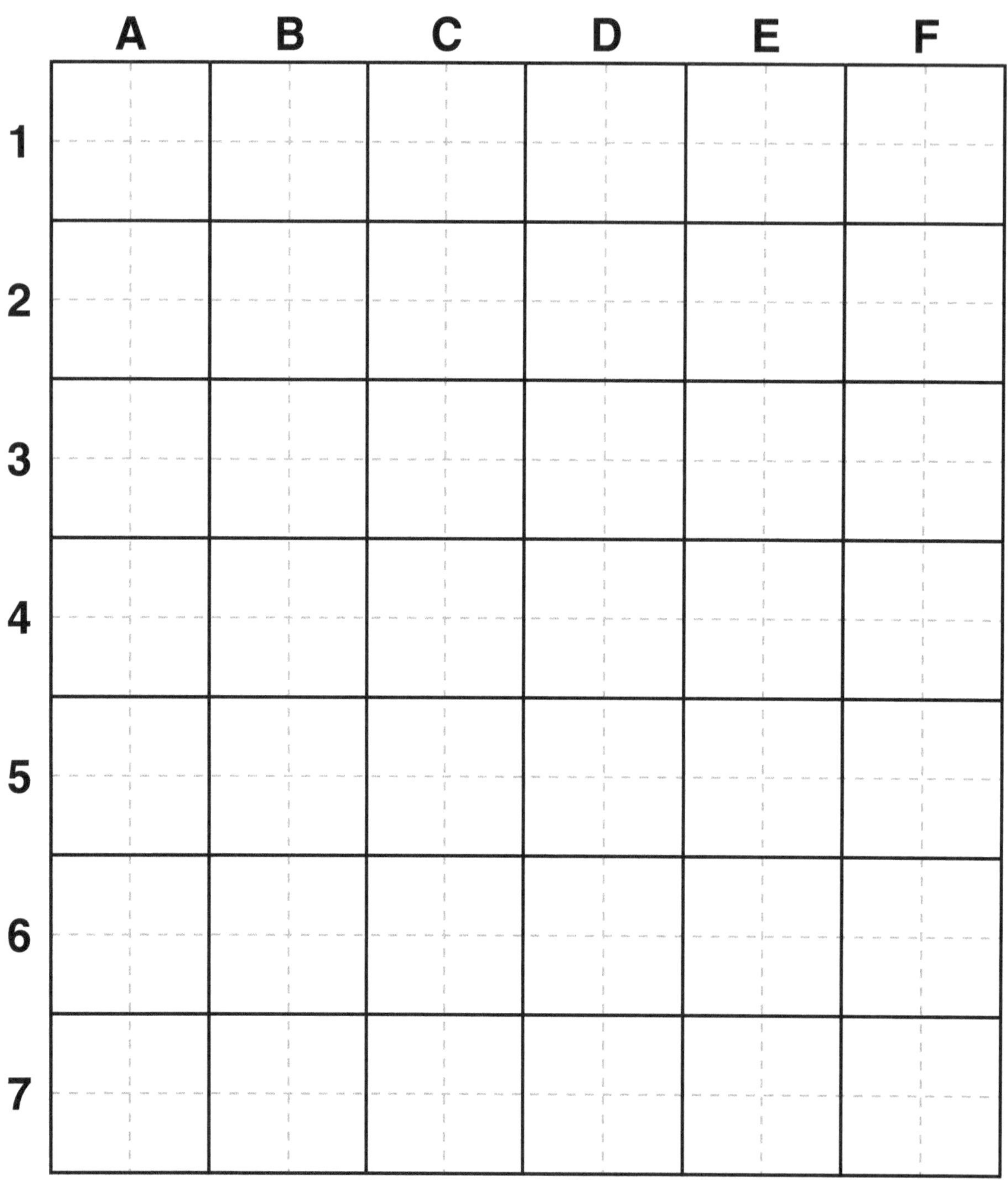

Coloring

Practice!

Make perfect!

Tracing

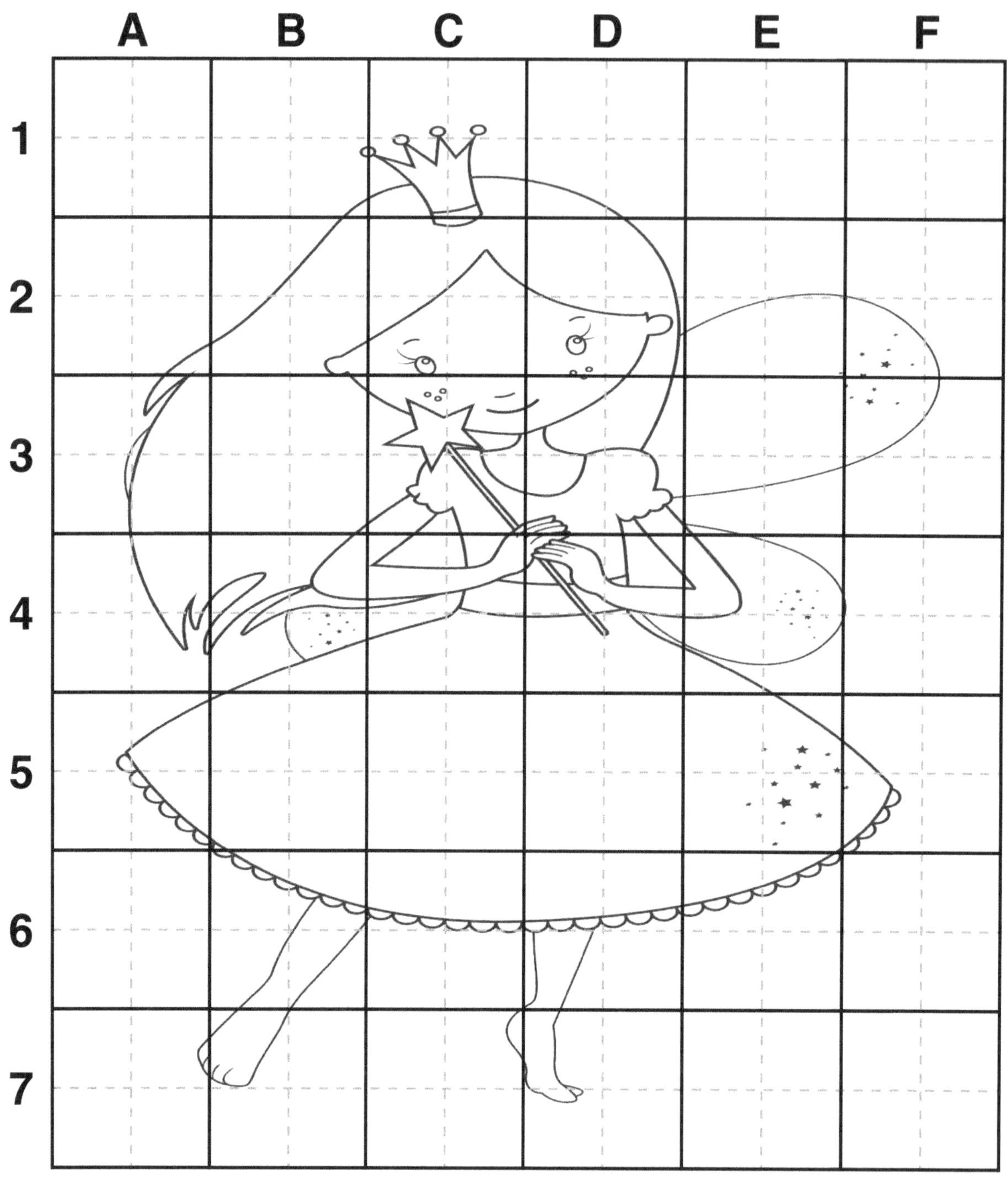

Your tract!

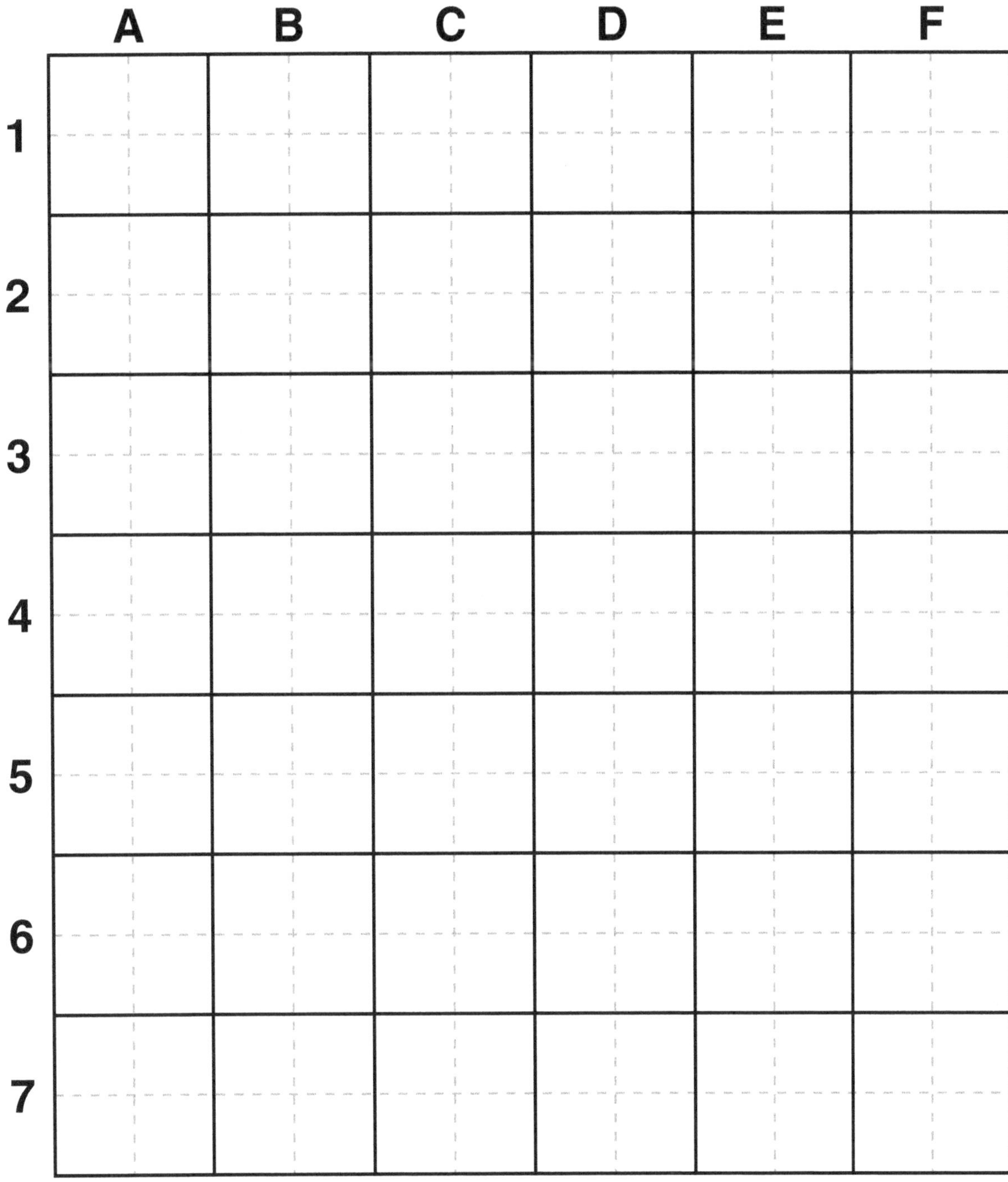

Coloring

Practice!

Make perfect!

Tracing

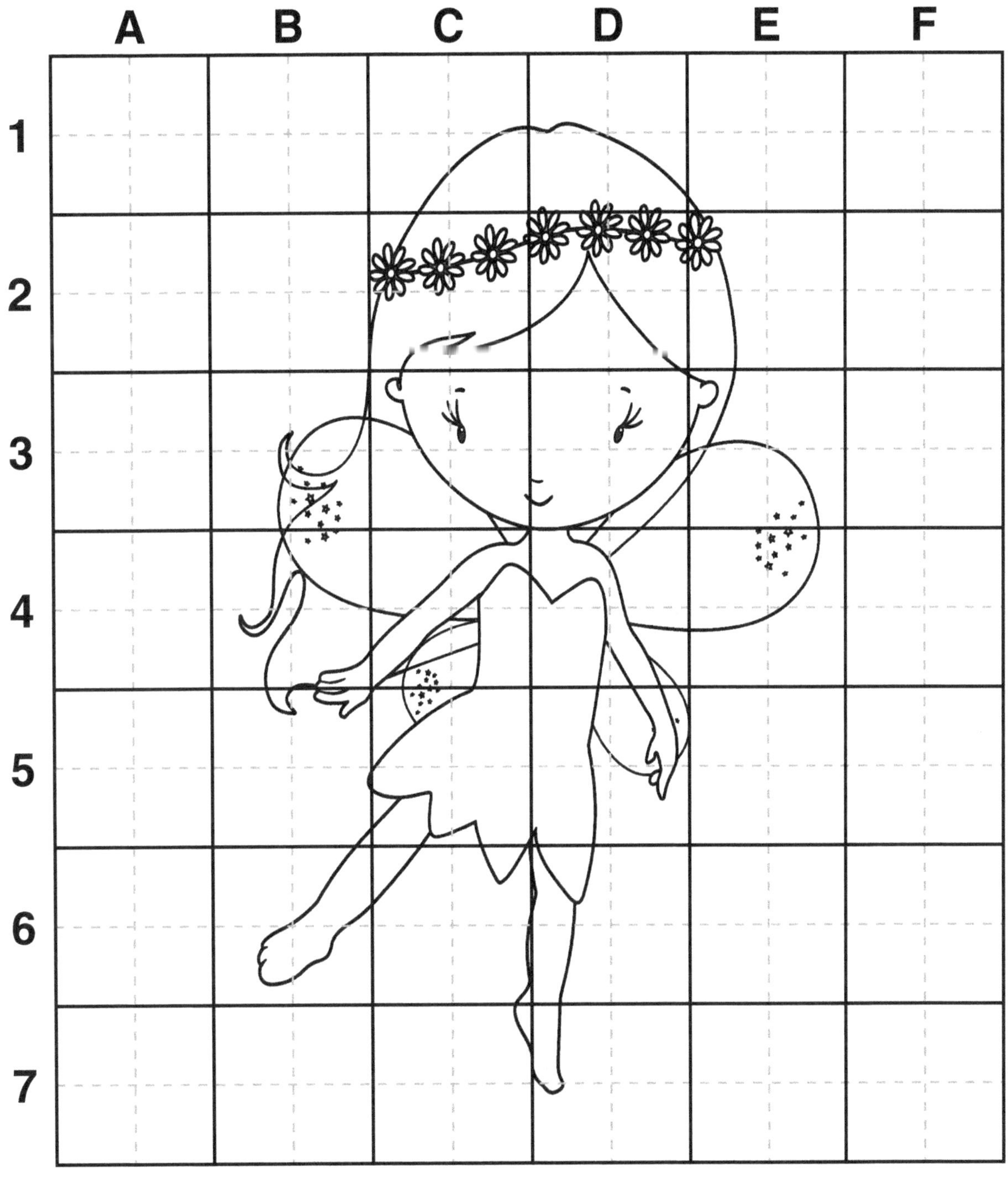

Your tract!

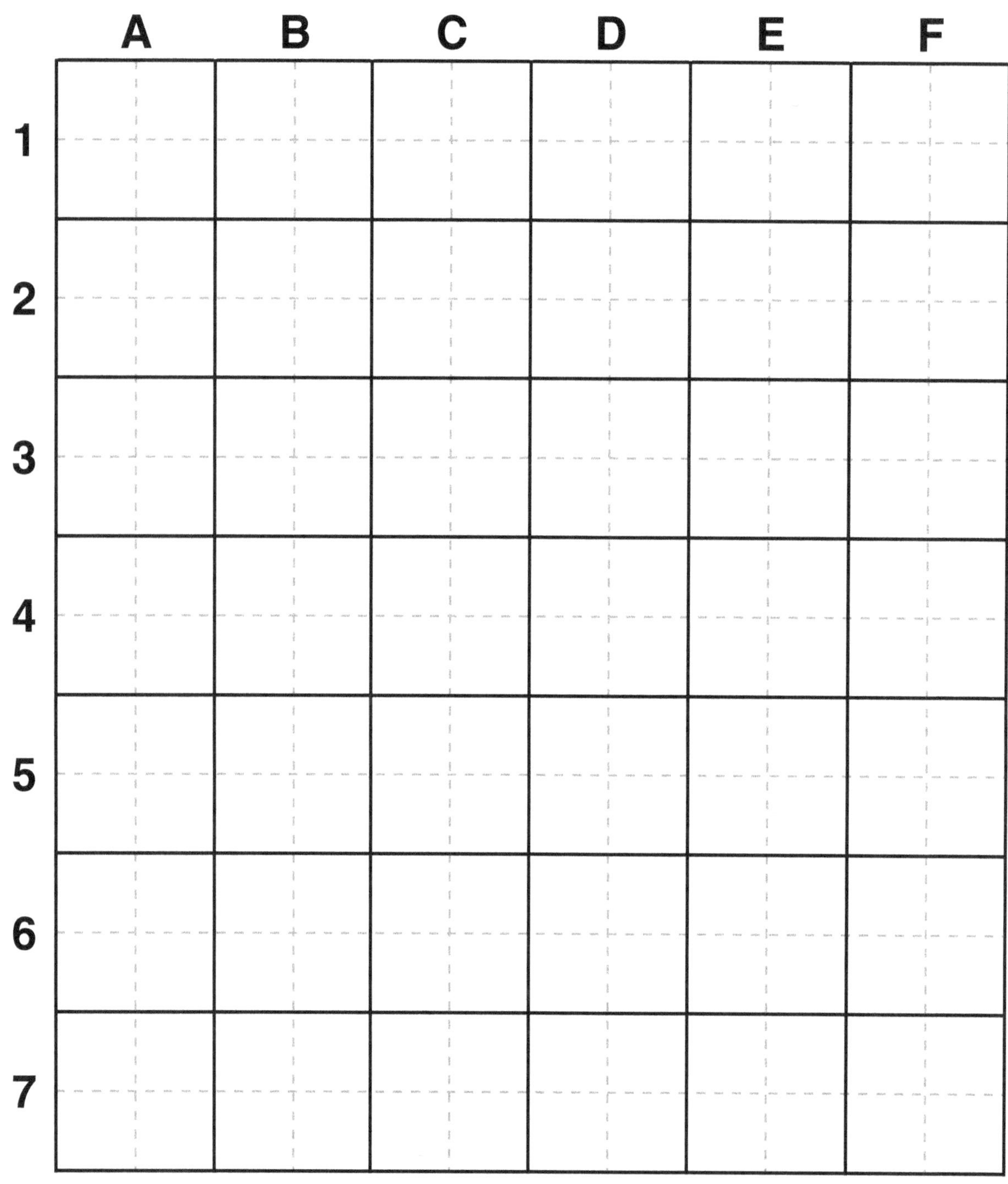

Coloring

Practice!

Make perfect!

Tracing

Your tract!

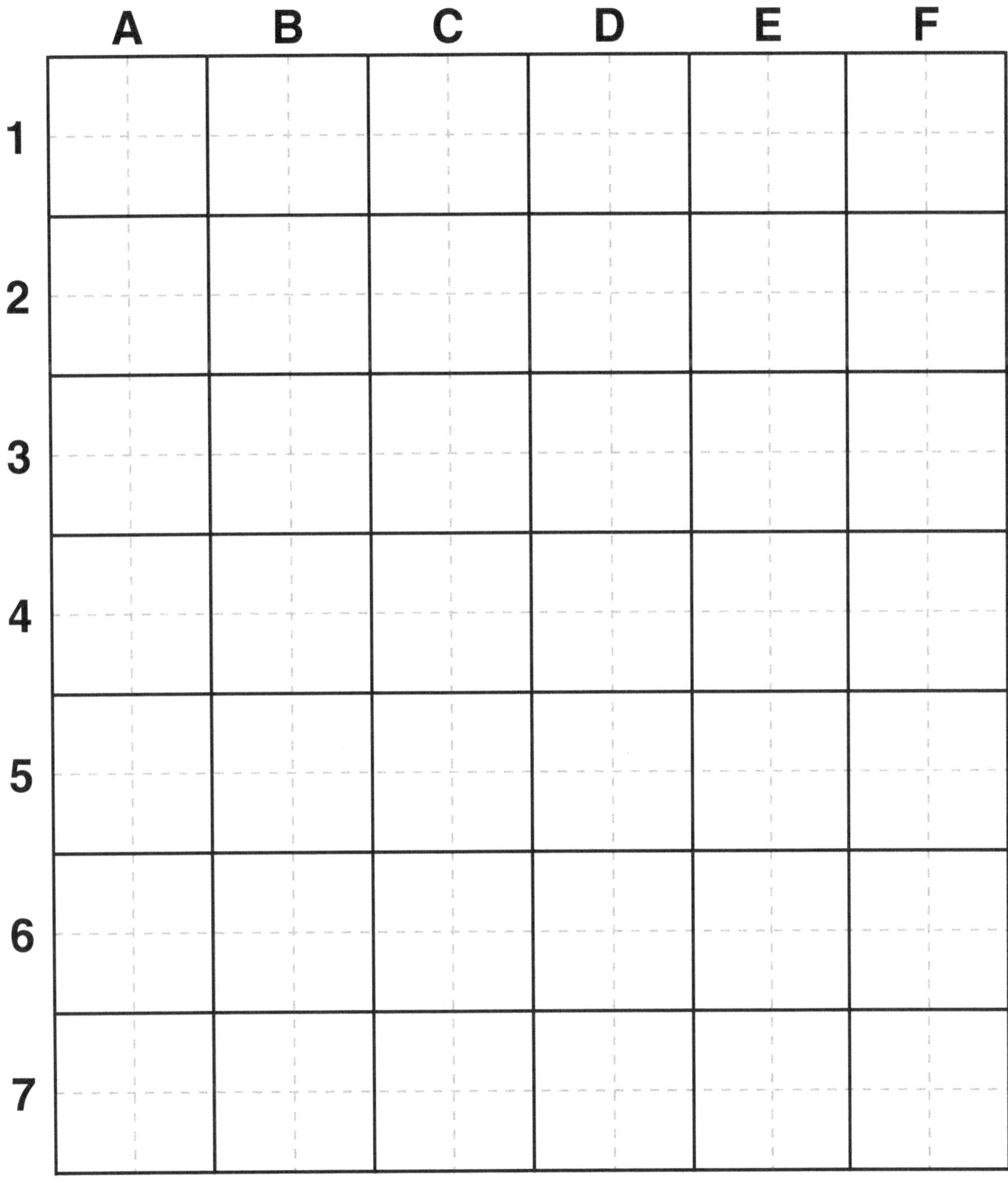

Coloring

Practice!

Make perfect!

Tracing

Your tract!

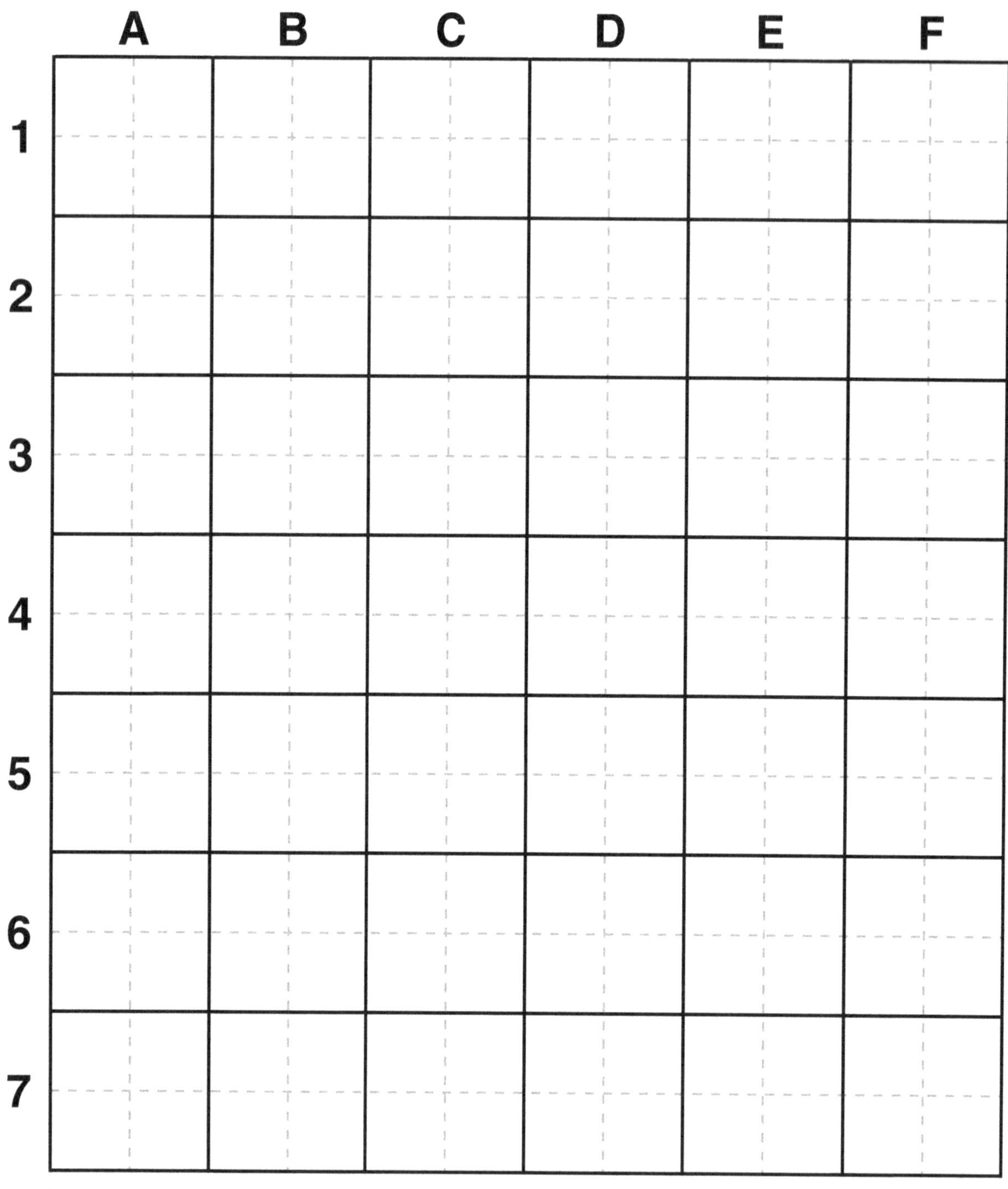

Coloring

Practice!

Make perfect!

Tracing

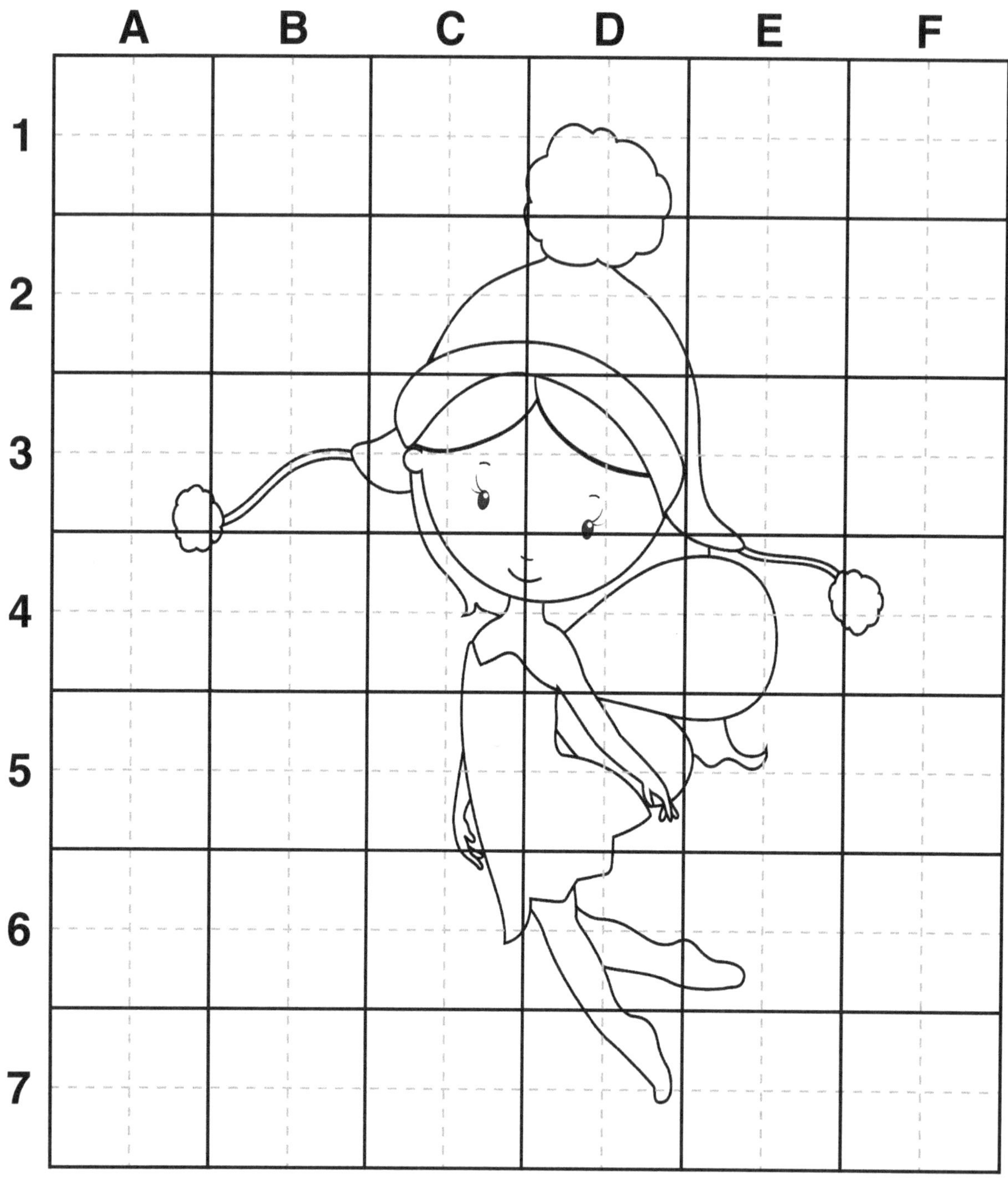

Your tract!

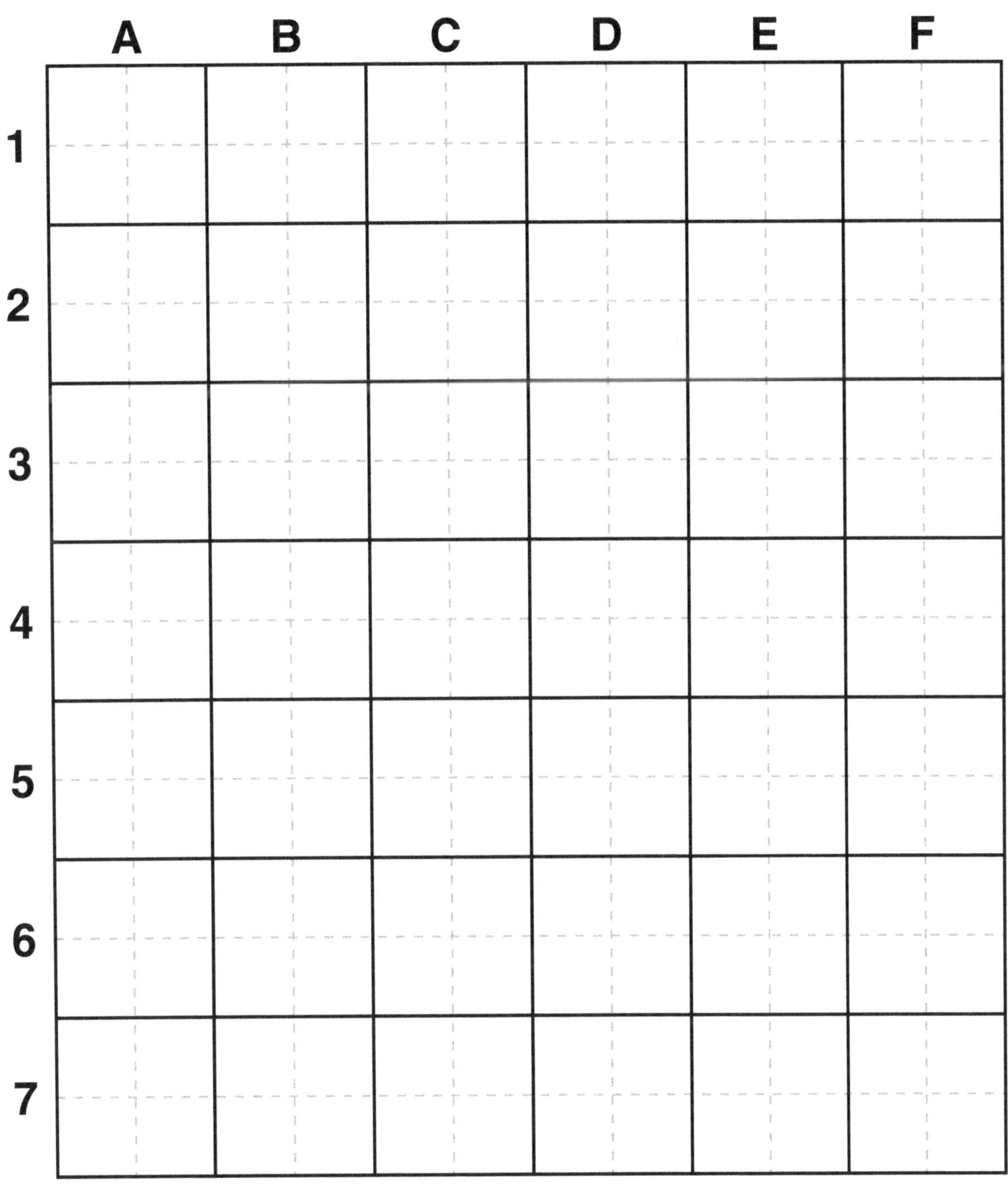

Coloring

Practice!

Make perfect!